RESEARCH BIBLIOGRAPHIES & CHECKLISTS

35

Aucassin et Nicolete: a critical bibliography

RESEARCH BIBLIOGRAPHIES & CHECKLISTS

RCB

General editors

A.D. Deyermond, J.R. Little and J.E. Varey

AUCASSIN ET NICOLETE

a critical bibliography

Barbara Nelson Sargent-Baur
and
Robert Francis Cook

Grant & Cutler Ltd
1981

© Grant & Cutler Ltd
1981

ISBN 0 7293 0108 7

I.S.B.N. 84-499-5180-1

DEPÓSITO LEGAL: V. 2.907-1981

Printed in Spain by Artes Gráficas Soler, S.A., Valencia
for

GRANT & CUTLER LTD
11, BUCKINGHAM STREET, LONDON, WC2

TABLE OF CONTENTS

Preface	7
Abbreviations	9
Editions	11
Selected Translations	29
Modern French	31
English	34
German	38
Other Languages	40
Dramatic Adaptations	42
Critical Studies	43
Author Index	77
Title Index	78
Subject Index	79
Index of Critics, Editors, Reviewers, Translators	81

PREFACE

Aucassin et Nicolete, like other works of medieval literature, began to emerge in the eighteenth century from that obscurity to which neo-classical taste had long relegated whatever partook of the "infélicité et calamité des Gothz". From its first translation into modern French in 1752, to its wide availability today in numerous editions and in translations into all the major European languages, it has come to enjoy a celebrity that seemingly was denied it in its own day. As it has attracted editors and translators and then readers, so too it has stimulated interpreters and commentators of many disciplines and persuasions. To follow the successive editions in which it has appeared, beginning in 1808, is to have a précis of the evolution of the theory and practice of deciphering, understanding and presenting a manuscript text. A survey of the interpretations and the studies of one or another aspect of this *chantefable*, which have followed the editions and in turn influenced succeeding ones, offers a paradigm of approaches to medieval literature over the past century.

It is, in fact, only slightly more than a century ago that the first major scholarly edition, that of Hermann Suchier, appeared, concurrently with the more popular one by Gaston Paris (with translation into modern French by Alexandre Bida). More than half a century has elapsed since F.W. Bourdillon published the last revision of his edition and brought his bibliography (mostly of editions, translations, and adaptations) up to about 1917. In 1925 Mario Roques issued, in the Classiques Français du Moyen Age, his first edition with an extensive critical bibliography; the latter was expanded in the revised second edition of 1929 and updated in the 1936 reprint. This remains the most widely used of scholarly editions. Since 1936 no comprehensive bibliography with commentary has been forthcoming. There is therefore, perhaps, justification for offering at the present time this new critical bibliography of all the important editions, translations, and studies of *Aucassin et Nicolete*. Its aim is to include all items published through 1978. One later item is also listed. All other publications on the subject will appear in a supplement to be published in due course.

Two hands have been at work here. The first section, treating editions and translations, was prepared by Robert Francis Cook; in his Introduction he gives an account of his inclusions and exclusions. In my own part of this enterprise, the Critical Studies, I have endeavoured to take note of all significant books, chapters of books, dissertations, articles, notes, review-articles, and miscellaneous treatments of the text. By "significant" I deliberately rule out all such marginalia as re-tellings for children, Graded French Readers, stage adaptations (e.g. those of Léon Riffard and of Sedaine), such imitations as *Ismir et Etoilette* of Mlle de Lubert, parodies such as *Marcassin et Tourlourette*, résumés and brief notices in encyclopedias and manuals of literary history, and the like. In principle, everything else has been included; and one can follow from year to year the types of response this work has generated. Romantic enthusiasm for spontaneous folk-expression, the lilies and langours of aesthetic criticism, rigorous paleographical and lexicographical analysis, broad considerations of intellectual and cultural history, debates on the nature of medieval literary genres, examinations of rhetorical conventions, statistical analysis, cryptology, source-studies (literary, historical, or anthropological), *Aucassin et Nicolete* as naïve and artless idyll, *Aucassin et Nicolete* as sophisticated parody – the winds of changing scholarly fashions have blown and will no doubt continue to blow on this slender, enigmatic, and fascinating text.

The order in each section is chronological, on the assumption that this is the arrangement that will most easily permit the reader to follow the preoccupations of scholars and the evolution in editorial and critical approaches over the years. Studies published in the same year are arranged alphabetically, as are the reviews given to a study. An alphabetical index at the end will facilitate the location of a particular editor, critic, or translator. There is also an index of subjects treated in the critical literature. Since *Aucassin et Nicolete* has not infrequently been discussed in connection with other literary works, a list of the latter is appended, as well as an index of authors.

The categories into which the Critical Studies are distributed are, admittedly, somewhat arbitrary. The distinctions between a simple summary review, a critical review, a review that touches on more than one study or edition, a review that includes some original scholarship, and a full-fledged review article, are not always easy to make. I have attempted by generous cross-references, and exceptionally by brief comments on a particular review, to shed light in amounts and directions that seemed appropriate. The editions and studies marked with an asterisk are those we have not been able to examine.

My thanks are due to the University of Pittsburgh, which has given encouragement to this project in the form of a Summer Research Grant, and to my husband for exemplary patience.

Barbara Nelson Sargent-Baur
University of Pittsburgh

ABBREVIATIONS

a) Journals and series:

ASNS	*Archiv für das Studium der neueren Sprachen und Literaturen*
BEC	*Bibliothèque de l'Ecole des Chartes*
CFMA	Classiques Français du Moyen Age
FR	*French Review*
FS	*French Studies*
LGRP	*Literaturblatt für germanische und romanische Philologie*
MA	*Le Moyen Age*
MLN	*Modern Language Notes*
MLR	*Modern Language Review*
MP	*Modern Philology*
R	*Romania*
RF	*Romanische Forschungen*
RLR	*Revue des Langues Romanes*
RN	*Romance Notes*
RPh	*Romance Philology*
RR	*Romanic Review*
SF	*Studi Francesi*
SP	*Studies in Philology*
UNCSRLL	University of North Carolina Studies in Romance Languages and Literatures
ZFSL	*Zeitschrift für französische Sprache und Literatur*
ZRP	*Zeitschrift für romanische Philologie*

b) Others:

BM	British Museum (now British Library)
BN	Bibliothèque Nationale
LC	Library of Congress
n.s.	new series
revd	revised
rpt	reprint

EDITIONS, TRANSLATIONS AND DRAMATIC ADAPTATIONS

by

Robert Francis Cook

A. EDITIONS

The various editions of *Aucassin et Nicolete* not only reflect the difficulty of interpreting a single manuscript as witness to a medieval text, but more precisely illustrate the limits of conjecture in dealing with any medieval French literary manuscript. It goes without saying that the copy of *AN* in BN Fr. 2168, fols 70-80, is faulty, as all handwritten books are. The intellectual problem lies in what the modern scholar is to do about that situation.

We should note at once that *AN* is outside the ambit of the greatest controversy in the history of textual criticism, the debate over combinatory method. Its subject was the propriety of mixing readings from several manuscript copies according to systematic judgements concerning the probability that each copy retains the author's own wording unchanged. A single copy offers no opportunity for such comparative, genealogical study, or for the establishment of a hierarchical stemma. If we may compare a given unique manuscript copy with one or more other copies of the same text, we increase thereby our chances – not our absolute certainty – of obtaining a correct text (to the extent that such a term has any meaning for a civilisation where imperfect transmission and faulty or incomplete copies were the expected norm). But even in the presence of several copies, the scholar may be unable to pronounce on the value of some of their readings. Experience has shown that scribes (naturally enough) made deliberate changes of various sorts in the texts they had before them, especially when the texts were popular literature in the vernacular.

It was long thought, and is still sometimes argued, that careful comparison of the manuscripts will unfailingly reveal which are copies of which others, or, more exactly, which ones derive at one or more removes from a common model. Reconstruction and comparison of those models might then allow elimination of the idiosyncratic errors they contain. This genealogical, combinatory method, often applied by pioneering medievalists, is associated with the name of Karl Lachmann, although he was not its inventor. Reliance instead on a single manuscript where others exist is an approach in turn linked with its proponent Joseph Bédier. Adherents of the older method will, of course, deplore the absence of other copies of *AN*, which might permit the creation of a genealogical chart and hence reveal by a process of elimination the words of the original text. Unfortunately, the more such family trees or stemmas are constructed, the more we learn about such chains of transmission, the more we realize they are usually too complex to allow determination of such questions from the evidence available to us. Scribes sometimes copied readings from more than one model into a single copy, which then belongs to no one family; it can be very hard to distinguish interpolations from omissions, given that some scribes were sensitive enough to disguise either process fairly well; the authors themselves sometimes intervened in the chain of transmission, making changes that then circulated in copies simultaneously with older readings; and in the absence of any notion of literary property, scribes and early readers alike made changes and corrections where the texts wrongly seemed unclear or illogical to them. Such early emendations will, of course, be in good Old French, and may be indistinguishable from the work of a first author. All of this means that the lack of a second or third copy of *AN*, while unfortunate, is less harmful than traditional pronouncements in matters of textual criticism might lead one to believe. What we might take for a correct reading in a second copy might well be no more than a medieval reader's conjecture, where medieval reader and modern editor alike have simply failed to grasp the intent of the original author's text.

The principal question facing the editor of *AN* then comes naturally from the preceding considerations. Is the editor to attempt first of all to understand and interpret the single flawed copy he has before him, or is he to assume, because he knows it is flawed, that he also knows how and where to correct it? The former procedure, dominant in the editing of *AN*, stems from a certain vision of the scholar as limited, in the search for authenticity, by lack of direct evidence, by incomplete access to the indirect evidence of medieval language and habits in general, and even by his own literary or historical prejudices. This attitude is usually called conservative, because it tends to preserve the text of the manuscript wherever it offers any chance of being right or even readable; the conservative editor usually corrects only hopeless scribal muddles, and then only with the greatest hesitation. Conjecture has little place in this method.

The opposite procedure, often recommended by reviewers but espoused only by Hermann Suchier and Gaston Paris among the principal scholarly editors of *AN*, implies a great confidence in the scholar's powers. Suitably trained and experienced, the interventionist editor deduces, from his knowledge of the literature and of the work in question, the correct state of the text wherever it appears corrupt. Sometimes such deductions are replaced by more or less pure conjectures; such was at first the case for the opening words of *AN*, where the manuscript's sequence *Del deport du viel antif* (1. 2) was rejected as unsuitable by several editors, and replaced in their versions by such combinations as *viel caitif* (Méon, emphatically); *tens antif* (Gaston Paris, in passing); or *duel caitif*

(Suchier, hesitantly). Upon examination by editors other than their inventors, these emendations have proven to be at least as problematical as the original manuscript reading.

The result of conservative editing is much like the work of a skilled but unimaginative medieval copyist, one who may or may not recognize flaws in what he is copying, but who does not attempt to remove them by any means at his disposal. The intervention of an editor, on the other hand, results in something more like the copy produced by an imaginative and independent-minded scribe, one who prefers an ideal state of the text – the one in his head – to the text delivered to him by the mechanisms of manuscript transmission. Needless to say, neither a scribe with ideas of his own nor an editor with imagination is precisely a substitute for the author. But by a curious paradox, the editor who emends his manuscript usually claims to produce, not a new text compounded of his own experience and conjectures, but rather a text more exactly like the author's. Unless we can thus purify the primary evidence, there is no reason to change what medieval civilisation produced. *AN*, in its single copy, furnishes an especially clear example of how these two attitudes toward textuality, toward scribes and toward authorship may yield different results in practice.

Thus Hermann Suchier treated a medieval French text with dramatic and parodic overtones, of uncertain date and undetermined origin, as though it were the product of a stable literary and linguistic culture, say a classical Latin work. The role of conjecture, in the case of a classical text (where scribal errors are often easily recognisable as departures from a known norm) is quite different from its role in the editing of a work in an unknown dialect, representing, in part at least, a lost spoken vernacular. By contrast with the conservative editions of Roques or Dufournet (and to some extent the earlier version given by Bourdillon) the Suchier texts, even the first, read somewhat differently from the manuscript both in form (the morphology and even the syntax of the original) and in substance (certain of its statements, thought unacceptable by Suchier and by his reviewers). Bourdillon counted thirty-seven arbitrary changes in Suchier's 1909 text. Even the literary form of the work inspired a typical series of revisions of the manuscript. In a minority of cases where the tag-lines or orphan lines found at the end of versified sections do not rhyme (or assonate) with the other lines in that position, Suchier (5th edition onwards) created new, rhyming lines out of Old French poetic elements known to him from other contexts – this although there is no other *chantefable* in existence, and thus no class of works from which to deduce the requirement that all verse sections in *chantefables* end with a rhyming line (cf. Roques, Aa30, p. xxi).

That it is fallacious thus to identify one's own linguistic and literary reactions absolutely with an author's, even after long study and preparation, was recognised fairly early in medieval studies, and despite the apparent paradox of reproducing a single manuscript known to be flawed, it is often thought today that any other course of action does not in fact give with certainty the result – a pure authorial text – that alone would justify our abandoning the only direct evidence we possess for the medieval text.

These general notions must nonetheless be somewhat modified in consideration of the case in hand. For *AN*, at least, the historical and literary dangers of modern intervention in the process of textual transmission have proven to be relatively small. At first glance, one might think its editorial history parallels closely the trends of textual criticism for the times of its editors. This impression is borne out in a general way by Roques's remarks in the preface to his edition (pp. xxvi-xxvii). Thus Suchier's work has acquired a reputation for hypercorrection, as befits the philosophy of a German scholar of the late nineteenth century. And Roques's version may be thought of as a reaction against archaic philologizing, as is so clearly the case in his edition of Chrétien de Troyes. But the details of the matter are complex, and deserve some comment.

First, in the absence of other manuscripts, it is always quite clear whose conjecture is involved when there is any deliberate departure from the reading of the copy in use. It is always the editor's guess, not the invention of a medieval reader or scribe or several generations of scribes; and Suchier was always scrupulously careful to indicate anything he rewrote in the known medieval text, as are his more conservative successors in those rarer instances when they too find the manuscript unreadable. Second, and perhaps more surprisingly, our text was given conservative treatment quite early in the history of modern editing, so that it was available as early as 1897 in something close to its manuscript form.

There are four major scholarly editions, i.e. those having historically and linguistically pertinent apparatus (introduction, notes, glossary, variants, tables), and resulting from a considered and systematic approach to the reproduction of the text. In chronological order of first publication, they are these.

Hermann Suchier's (1878-1933), eleven states, of which no two are identical (the sixth, seventh and eighth are practically the same for the text), representing a series of attempts to reach a definitive corrected text with something of a variant-reading apparatus. The method is generally deductive and at times conjectural. Suchier sometimes maintained and sometimes rejected his own emendations over the years, so that the relationships among the texts are complex. The first eight editions are the work of Hermann Suchier himself. The ninth through the eleventh were revised in part by his son Walther (who used Bourdillon's facsimile, Ab1 below, and not the manuscript as his father had done in the first instance at least). Brief introduction; list of abbreviations and disagreements with previous editions; variants; notes; dialect study; partial grammar ("Paradigmen"); glossary; tables of names and (at first) assonances, and later a reproduction of the music, which is preserved. Walther Suchier gives a lengthy literary introduction in the ninth and tenth editions.

Francis William Bourdillon's (1887-1919). There was a false start, in which Bourdillon followed Suchier's second edition, with occasional recourse to Paris (Aa7) or Moland (Aa5), and to a certain number of personal conjectures, mostly conservative. Bourdillon then gave, in 1897, a remarkably faithful edition of the text, quite the equal of Roques's in thoroughness and nearly its equal in methodological rigour (if not in linguistic science). From the first edition, Bourdillon professed principles of translation that are quite similar to those usually held now. None of Bourdillon's introductory or critical material is beneath scholarly notice today, though Suchier and Roques used his work very sparingly, and Dufournet does not cite him at all. Bourdillon revised his text relatively little in the later editions, but modified his introduction twice (1897, 1919), and regularly updated his bibliography. Critical material varies from text to text, but always includes introduction, glossary, and bibliography.

Mario Roques's (1925-29, often reprinted), conservative in method and more successful in explaining why the medieval text reads as it does. Now considered the standard edition. Briefer than Suchier's in the supporting material. Full introduction, including remarks on language and versification; bibliography; notes, table of names, glossary.

Jean Dufournet's (1973), the result of a new conservative reading of the manuscript, and necessarily much like Roques's, except in details of punctuation; indeed the two most recent editions are practically identical in substance, by virtue of their common method. Full introduction, bibliography, notes (including some glosses). We may compare the treatment Dufournet gives the lengthy prose section XXIV, including the dialogue between Aucassin and the herdsman, with the treatment given it by Roques. Dufournet replaces Roques's semi-colons with periods in 14, 29, 79, and 87 (reference is to the division by lines in Roques), and with commas in 9, 52 and 53; conversely, Dufournet has a period for Roques's colon in 38. The comma splicing two complete sentences in 50, present in every edition since Méon (semi-colon in Bourdillon), is retained. In the matter of morphology, Dufournet maintains the MS reading *li mellor* in 51 (a subject article used with a direct object), where Roques corrects to *le* (as had Suchier and Bourdillon before him). Keeping his non-specialist audience in mind, Dufournet supplies (after Suchier) conjectural text (imitated from XIX) in 72-4, where the MS is damaged. He once accents monosyllabic *nes* 'nose'. In other respects, Roques and Dufournet agree exactly; we may compare Suchier's four substantive and nine formal emendations for this same passage in his eighth edition.

It should be noted that every one of the major editors made significant contributions to the study of the text. Suchier and Bourdillon in particular were better paleographers than any of their predecessors. Especially where the lexicon is concerned, none of the editions should be entirely neglected, whatever one's reaction to the edited text as primary material.

The reader will have concluded, with some considerable justification, that in the case of *AN*, the various editorial approaches have led to the creation of generally similar texts. Except for Suchier's most heavily corrected versions (especially editions 2-9), the major modern editions have reproduced the manuscript with accuracy overall. That does not mean it is a matter of total indifference which edition is being considered. The student of *Aucassin et Nicolete*, in dealing with the scholarly literature concerning this *chantefable*, should recall that studies and articles on it will have been influenced at least subtly by the state of the text appearing in the edition used. Even where substantive readings are not under discussion, the early editors' habit of altering the manuscript's linguistic forms should not be forgotten. Especially before the appearance of Roques's first edition (1925), or before its acceptance as standard, it is important to ascertain which of the varying versions of Suchier or Bourdillon was used by an earlier scholar.

As has been noted, Bourdillon's second edition, though not his first, was based on a new reading of the manuscript; it was not changed substantially in any of its reprintings after its first appearance in 1897. Suchier's first edition, while not a faithful reproduction of the manuscript text, is closer to it than any of his others. The second through the eighth all show considerable reliance upon the conjectures of other editors (including Karl Bartsch in his *Chrestomathie de l'ancien français* (Leipzig: E.C.W. Vogel, 1866; many revd eds) and upon the recommendations of various reviewers, especially Adolf Tobler and Gaston Paris. Thus in XIV, 19-22 (Aucassin's description of women's love as merely physical), Hermann Suchier never accepted the MS reading *en son oeul* 'in her eye', preferring to correct *en son l'oeul* 'on top of her eye' for the sake of a presumed parallel with the two phrases following. Bourdillon, Roques and Dufournet all reject that emendation. But in the same sentence, Suchier at first gave the MS reading *en son le cateron de sa mamele*, and corrected this legitimate Picardism to *en son le teteron*, a typical editors' *lectio facilior*, only at the instigation of Hugo Andresen (see Suchier's ref., C8) and Gaston Paris (see Aa8.1 and Aa13.1). Walther Suchier retained the *lectio facilior* in the ninth edition, then returned in the tenth to the MS reading, thus completing the critical circle (the Andresen emendation still appears as a variant). Walther Suchier's final text (1932) exhibits generally a more conservative attitude – indeed, Eugen Lerch suggests in his review (see Aa27.1, below) that he seems to have used Roques – so that the tenth Suchier edition, and the *editio minor* I have called the eleventh, are exceptions in the forty-six-year span of the series.

All of the preceding remarks are of necessity quite general; precise comparison of the editors' work is best carried out through detailed examination of each editor's critical apparatus, a process beyond the scope of this volume. A few final points concerning the value of the various editions for the user may, however, be quickly made. First, despite their interest for the history of textual criticism, the value of Bourdillon's early conservative attitude, and of Suchier's (where it is manifest), is limited by the restricted access to Old French texts which was normal at that time. Roques is able to explain some forms and readings rejected by most or all of his predecessors (*le cuer m'esclaire*, III, 16; *creutes*, VI, 28; *le cateron de sa mamele*, already cited) because the language and dialect of the text are better understood in his time. Changing scholarly conceptions of the work's sense have also influenced the editing of the text. Where scholars once thought of it as naïve and idealistic, it is now generally agreed that the *chantefable* contains important elements of irony and comedy. Bourdillon, Roques and Dufournet have been able to call upon those elements to justify many inconsistencies, especially illogical dialogue.

Though Roques's critical material appears quite brief in comparison with Suchier's, that is in part because he does not note all graphic peculiarities, stray letters, superscriptions and the like, as Suchier scrupulously does. Roques silently corrects a certain number of errors thought by all editors to be obvious ones. His glossary is the most nearly complete to date. For fuller information on some points, Dufournet's more recent notes should be consulted; they are the result of an exemplary search of the secondary literature. Let us note in particular that Dufournet is able to justify retention of the interjection *aioire* in X, 60, on the basis of Roques's work done after Roques had completed his own edition (cf. Aa30, pp. e-f).

Suchier's various editions contain a skeleton Old French grammar for the use of students approaching that language for the first time through *AN*. Although Suchier's is intelligently drafted to take into account the peculiar linguistic features of *AN* – at least the ones he allowed to remain in the text – the fact remains that a copy like Fr. 2168, in which dialect features are strongly marked and are to some extent mixed, is a confusing starting point for beginners. Such grammars are now rarely used, and indeed no longer correspond to the linguists' conception of Old French dialects. We must not be misled by

Hermann Suchier's claim (not made by Walther Suchier) that his edition is not critical with respect to scribal language forms. Hermann Suchier in fact corrects graphies fairly often, if not systematically. His principle for the treatment of scribal forms, while revealing of the interventionist attitudes mentioned at the beginning of this essay, is not entirely clear: "Nur was auch im Sinne des Schreibers unrichtig zu nennen war ist korrigiert worden, während Sprachformen, welche sich nur durch verjüngende oder mundartliche Umgestaltungen von den ursprünglichen unterscheiden, unangetastet blieben" (1st ed., p. 73). How one enters into the scribe's mind, and how one recognizes dialect transformations of the lost original, are not explained. Finally, Suchier's discussion of the scribe's dialect does not always account for the difference between graphy and spoken form, while Roques's does.

It is a pleasure to express my gratitude to the staff of the Alderman Library of the University of Virginia, and especially to the Interlibrary Loan Department, for their efficient aid in obtaining widely scattered editions and translations of *Aucassin et Nicolete.*

Aa. THE EDITED OLD FRENCH TEXT

Order is chronological; only complete texts and not anthologized excerpts are included.

Aa1 [1808 Méon]. *Fabliaux et contes des poètes françois des XI, XII, XIII, XIV et XVe siècles, tirés des meilleurs auteurs.* Publiés par [Etienne] Barbazan. Nouvelle édition, augmentée et revue sur les manuscrits de la Bibliothèque Impériale par M. [Dominique] Méon. 4 vols. Paris: B. Warée Oncle, 1808.
See also Aa2-4. Old French text (much emended) with musical notation: I, pp. 380-418. See C3.

Aa2* [1826? Méon]. *Livre mignard, ou la Fleur des fabliaux.* Ed. Charles Malo. Paris: Librairie Universelle [1826?].
Méon's text (Aa1). Publication data uncertain; LC gives Librairie Universelle as pub.; Quérard gives Janet as pub. and 1826 as date; BM gives 1825 as date; BN lacks; *Bibl. de la France* lacks for those dates.

Aa3* [1829 Méon]. *Fabliaux ou contes, fables et romans du XIIe et du XIIIe siècle.* Trans. Jean-Baptiste Legrand d'Aussy. 3rd ed. 5 vols. Paris: Renouard, 1829.
Méon's text (Aa1): III, appendice, pp. 9-25. Cf. Ba2.

Aa4* [1842 Méon]. Ideler, Julius Ludwig. *Geschichte der altfranzösischen National-Literatur von den ersten Anfängen bis auf Franz I.* Berlin: Naucksche Buchhandlung, 1842.
Méon's text (Aa1): pp. 317-42.

Aa5 [1856 Moland]. *Nouvelles françoises en prose du XIII^{e}siècle, publiées d'après les manuscrits...* avec une introduction et des notes, par MM. [Louis] Moland et C[harles] d'Héricault. Bibliothèque Elzévirienne, LXV. Paris: P. Jannet, 1856.
Text, pp. 231-310, with musical notation and explanatory notes. Literary remarks, pp. xxxvii-xliii. Accepts many emendations of Méon's (Aa1).

Aa6 [1866 Moland]. *Aucassin et Nicolette, roman de chevalerie provençal-picard.* Publié avec introduction et traduction par Alfred Delvau. Paris: Bachelin-Deflorenne, 1866.

Text similar or identical to Moland's (Aa5) and surely derived from it. Minimal punctuation. 150 copies only. Musical notation. Text in bastard Gothic; amplified translation beneath. Cf. Ba4.

Aa7 [1878 Paris]. *Aucassin et Nicolette, chantefable du douzième siècle.* Traduite par A[lexandre] Bida. Révision du texte original et préface par Gaston Paris. Paris: Hachette, 1878. xxxi + 104 pp.

Emended text, similar in the main to Moland (Aa5), collated with the manuscript, and having no critical apparatus. Some typographical errors. Translation incomplete (p. xxi). Bida's liminary poem bears the date of January 12, 1871. Preface by Gaston Paris rpt (partially) in *Poemes et légendes* (C9). Cf. Ba5.

Reviews: .1 Gaston Raynaud, *BEC*, XL (1879), 96-100.
.2 Hermann Suchier, *Allgemeine Zeitung* (Dec. 1, 1878).
See also Aa8.1.

Aa8 [1878 Suchier[1]]. *Aucassin und Nicolete.* Neu nach der Handschrift mit Paradigmen und Glossar von Hermann Suchier. Paderborn: Ferdinand Schöningh, 1878. 116pp.

Reviews: .1 Gaston Paris, *R*, VIII (1879), 284-93 (Compares with Aa7).
.2 Gaston Raynaud, *BEC*, XL (1879), 96-100.
*.3 Edmund Stengel, *Jenaer Literaturzeitung* (March 15, 1879).
.4 Adolf Tobler, *ZRP*, II (1878), 624-9.

Aa9 [1881 Suchier[2]]. *Aucassin und Nicolete.* Neu nach der Handschrift mit Paradigmen und Glossar von Hermann Suchier. Zweite Auflage. Paderborn: Schöningh, 1881. 116pp.

Cf. Bb5.

Reviews: .1 A.M. Elliott, *American Journal of Philology,* II (1881), 234-6.
*.2 John Koch, *LGRP*, II (1881), 248.
*.3 Karl Vollmöller, *Zeitschrift die Gegenwart,* XXX (1881).
*.4 Ernst Weber, *Deutsche Literaturzeitung* (1881), 1546.

Aa10 [1887 Bourdillon[1]]. *Aucassin and Nicolette. A Love Story.* Edited in Old French and Rendered in Modern English, with Introduction, Glossary, etc., by F[rancis] W[illiam] Bourdillon, M.A., Oxon. London: Kegan Paul, Trench, and Co., 1887. lxxxii + 245pp.

Text done without benefit of the manuscript. Musical notation; five appendices; bibliography; glossary.

Aa11 [1889 Suchier[3]]. *Aucassin und Nicolete.* Neu nach der Handschrift mit Paradigmen und Glossar von Hermann Suchier.

Dritte Auflage. Paderborn: Schöningh, 1889. 118pp.
Reviews: .1 Alfred Schulze, *ASNS*, LXXXIV (1890), 455.
.2 Maurice Wilmotte, *MA*, III (1890), 20-30.

Aa12 [1897 Bourdillon[2]]. *Aucassin and Nicolette: An Old-French Love Story.* Edited and Translated by Francis William Bourdillon, M.A. Second Edition. The Text Collated Afresh with the Manuscript at Paris, the Translation Revised and the Introduction Rewritten. London and New York: Macmillan, 1897. lxxii + 229pp.
See also Aa15, Aa20, Aa21, Aa26, Aa40. Musical notation; notes; appendices; bibliography; glossary.

Aa13* [1899 Suchier[4]]. *Aucassin und Nicolete.* Mit Paradigmen und Glossar von Hermann Suchier. Vierte Auflage. Paderborn: Schöningh, 1899. 120pp.
Reviews: .1 Gaston Paris, *R*, XXIX (1900), 287-92; cf. Paris's preliminary remarks, *R*, XXVIII (1899), 643.
.2 Alfred Schulze, *ASNS*, CII (1899), 224.

Aa14 [1903 Suchier[5]]. *Aucassin et Nicolette.* Texte critique accompagné de paradigmes et d'un lexique par Hermann Suchier. Cinquième édition, partiellement refondue. Traduite en français par Albert Counson. Paderborn: Schöningh; Paris: J. Gamber, 1903. 131pp.
The Old French text is not translated.
Review: .1 Wendelin Foerster, "Randglossen zur Cantefable," C14; see Suchier's reply, C15.

Aa15* [1903 Bourdillon[2]]. *C'est d'Aucassin et de Nicolete.* [London: Eragny Press, 1903.] 55pp.
Text: Bourdillon[2] (Aa12) with some revisions by the editor; 230 copies only. Vale type, design by Lucien Pissaro.

Aa16* [1906 Suchier[6]]. *Aucassin et Nicolette.* Texte critique accompagné de paradigmes et d'un lexique par Hermann Suchier. Sixième édition partiellement refondue. Traduction française par Albert Counson. Paderborn: Schöningh, 1906. 133pp.
Review: .1 Antoine Thomas, *R*, XXXVI (1907), 147-8.

Aa17* [1909 Suchier[7]]. *Aucassin et Nicolette.* Texte critique accompagné de paradigmes et d'un lexique par Hermann Suchier. Septième édition avec une table contenant la

notation musicale. Traduction française par Albert Counson. Paderborn: Schöningh, 1909. 134pp.
Review: .1 [Heinrich Morf], *ASNS*, CXX (1908), 249-50.

Aa18 [1911 Tournoux]. *Aucassin et Nicolette.* [Ed. Georges A. Tournoux. Leipzig: Ernst Kowohlt, 1911.] 78pp.
This edition, essentially quite conservative, has rarely been taken into account in the treatment of the text, for it is virtually unreadable. It is printed in the *civilité* typeface, and one can imagine the combined effect of uncertain Old French dialect with a type form artificially derived from a Baroque calligraphic style. Even the colophon, in Modern French, is rarely transcribed with accuracy although it is printed in textura Gothic; it reads:

> Edité par Georges A. Tournoux et tiré à deux cent cinquante exemplaires numérotés ce livre a été achevé d'imprimer le xx août MCMXI par Joh. Enschedé en Zonen à Haarlem pour la maison Ernest Kowohlt de Leipzig.

Aa19 [1913 Suchier[8]]. *Aucassin et Nicolette.* Texte critique accompagné de paradigmes et d'un lexique par Hermann Suchier. Huitième édition avec une table contenant la notation musicale. [Trans. Albert Counson.] Paderborn: Schöningh, 1913. 136pp.
See also Aa23, Aa29.

Aa20* [1917 Bourdillon[2]]. *Aucassin and Nicolette. An Old-French Love-Story*. Edited and Translated by Francis William Bourdillon. Second Edition. The Text Collated Afresh With the Manuscript at Paris, the Translation Revised and the Introduction Rewritten. Manchester: The University Press; London: Longmans, 1917. lxxii + 229pp.
Re-issue of Aa12.

Aa21 [1919 Bourdillon[3]]. *Aucassin et Nicolete.* Edited by F.W. Bourdillon, M.A. Manchester: The University Press; London: Longmans, Green and Co. 1919. xxxviii + 120pp.
Revd text, notes and glossary, new introduction, updated bibliography. Translation omitted. See also Aa26, Aa40.
Review: .1 E.G.R. Waters, *MLR*, XV (1920), 192-8.

Aa22 [1921 Suchier[9]]. *Aucassin und Nicolette.* Kritischer Text mit Paradigmen und Glossar von Hermann Suchier. Neunte Auflage bearbeitet von Walther Suchier. Paderborn: Schöningh, 1921. 111pp.

Introduction (60pp.) by Walther Suchier.
Review: *.1 [Eugen] Lerch, *LGRP*, XLIV, 1-2 (1923), 24-31.

NOTE. 1921 P.A. Guiton is not an edition, despite the title-page, but an adaptation for classroom use (see Ba7).

Aa23 [1923 Suchier[8]]. *Aucassin et Nicolette.* Texte critique accompagné de paradigmes et d'un lexique par Hermann Suchier. Huitième édition avec une table contenant la notation musicale. [Trans. Albert Counson.] New York: G.E. Stechert, 1923.
Cf. Aa19.

Aa24 [1925 Roques[1]]. *Aucassin et Nicolette. Chantefable du XIIIe siècle.* Editée par Mario Roques. CFMA, [XLI]. Paris: Champion, 1925. xxxvi + 97pp.
Full introduction, including bibliography; facsimile; notes, table of names, glossary.
Reviews: .1 [Léon Clédat], *Revue de Philologie française*, XXXVIII (1926), 82-3.
.2 T. Atkinson Jenkins, *MP*, XXV (1927-8), 120.
.3 Walther Suchier, *ZFSL*, L (1927), 166-70.

Aa25 [1929 Roques[2]]. *Aucassin et Nicolette. Chantefable du XIIIe siècle.* Editée par Mario Roques. Deuxième édition revue. Paris: Champion, 1929. xxxviii + 105pp.
Expanded bibliography. Revd glossary. The 2nd revd ed. reported by LC under the serial number NA 0489706 and dated 1925 is surely this ed. See also Aa30.

Aa26 [1930 Bourdillon[3]]. *Aucassin et Nicolete.* Edited by F.W. Bourdillon. Manchester: University Press, 1930.
Reprint of Bourdillon's third edition (Aa21).

Aa27 [1932 Suchier[10]]. *Aucassin und Nicolette.* Kritischer Text mit Paradigmen und Glossar, von Hermann Suchier. Zehnte Auflage bearbeitet von Walther Suchier. Paderborn: Schöningh, 1932. lix + 115pp.
Review: *.1 Eugen Lerch, *LGRP*, LV, 7-8 (1934), 247-53.

Aa28 [1932 (1933)Suchier[11]]. *Aucassin und Nicolette.* Textausgabe nebst Paradigmen und Glossar. Bearbeitet von Walther Suchier. Paderborn: Schöningh, 1932 [1933]. 76pp.
Text from Suchier[10] (1932) with variants, paradigms and glossary only (notes omitted).

NOTE. 1933 E.B. Williams is not an edition, despite the title page, but a school version of Bida's translation (see Ba10).

Aa29* [1936 Suchier[8]]. *Aucassin et Nicolette.* Texte critique accompagné de paradigmes et d'un lexique, par Hermann Suchier. Huitième édition avec une table contenant la notation musicale. [Trans. Albert Counson.] New York: G.E. Stechert, 1936. xiii + 136pp.
Cf. Aa19.

Aa30 [1936 Roques[2]]. *Aucassin et Nicolette. Chantefable du XIIIe siècle.* Editée par Mario Roques. Deuxième édition. Nouveau tirage revu et complété. Paris: Champion, 1935. xxxviii + 105pp.
Unrevised photographic reprint of Roques's second edition (1929) with a supplementary gathering *a-g* at end, giving new notes, some additions and modifications to the glossary, and additional entries for the bibliography (through 1935). See also Aa36-9, Aa41; these reprints are issued under their dates of reprinting (1954, 1962, 1965, 1967, 1975), as is Champion's practice for the CFMA. They lack the facsimile. The "third edition" catalogued by LC under serial number NA 0489713 is surely the 1936 reprint. See also the supplement to this ed. published in article form in 1955 (C79).

Aa31* [1936 Roques[2]A]. *C'est d'Aucassin et de Nicolete. Aucassin et Nicolette.* Chantefable du XIIIe siècle transcrite d'après le manuscrit de la Bibliothèque Nationale par Mario Roques, avec une traduction du XVIIIe siècle par La Curne de Sainte Palaye. Ymages et ornemens par Joseph Hémard. Paris; Librairie Lutetia, 1936.
Roques's text (Aa24-5).

Aa32* [1937 Linker]. *Aucassin et Nicolete.* Edited by Robert White Linker. Chapel Hill, North Carolina; n. pub., 1937. 43pp.
A mimeographed preliminary version of Aa35, presumably for use in the classroom.

Aa33 [1939 Pauphilet]. *Aucassin et Nicolette,* in *Poètes et romanciers du Moyen Age.* Texte établi et annoté par Albert Pauphilet. Bibliothèque de la Pléïade, LII. Paris: Gallimard, 1939. Rpt 1952.
Text, pp. 451-82. Glossed. Graphies of text often altered, presumably to facilitate reading.

Aa34 [1946 Thomov].

ОКАСИН И НИКОЛЕТА

СТАРОФРЕНСКА ПЕСЕН-РАЗКАЗ ОТ XIII^{в}

УВОД, ТЕКСТ И ПРЕВОД, С ДВЕ ФАКСИМИЛЕТА, БЕЛЕЖКИ, РЕЧНИК И ПОКАЗАЛЕЦ НА СОБСТВЕНИТЕ ЛИЧНИ И МЕСТНИ ИМЕНА

ОТ

ТОМА СТ. ТОМОВ

Aucassin et Nicolette. Chantefable du XIIIe siècle. Avec introduction, texte et traduction bulgare en regard, deux facsimilés, notes, glossaire et index des noms propres de personnes et de lieux, par Thomas S. Thomov. Bibliothèque de l'Université [of Sofia], CCCXVII. Sofia: Presses Universitaires, 1946. lii + 140pp.

All accompanying material in Bulgarian. A very conservative transcription, virtually identical to Roques's (Aa30) except for a few misreadings or misprints and widely scattered emendations.

Aa35 [1948 Linker]. *Aucasssin et Nicolete.* Edited by Robert White Linker. Chapel Hill: University of North Carolina Press [1948]. viii + 49pp.

Music: bibliography (five items). Classroom text (cf. Aa32).

Aa36* [1954 Roques[2]]. See Aa30.

Aa37* [1962 Roques[2]]. See Aa30.

Aa38 [1965 Roques[2]]. See Aa30.

Aa39 [1967 Roques[2]]. See Aa30.

Aa40 [1970 Bourdillon[3]]. Rpt of Aa21; cf. Aa26.

Aa41 [1973 Dufournet]. *Aucassin et Nicolette.* Edition critique. Chronologie, préface, bibliographie, traduction et notes par Jean Dufournet. Paris: Garnier-Flammarion, 1973. 191pp.

Brief reviews: .1 Gianni Mombello, *SF*, XVIII (1974), 131.
.2 Michel Rousse, *RLR*, LXXXI (1974), 543-4.

Aa42* [1975 Roques[2]]. See Aa30.

Ab. FACSIMILE

Ab1 *CEST DAUCASĪ 7 DE NICOLETE.* Reproduced in Photo-Facsimile and Type-Transliteration From the Unique MS. in the Bibliothèque Nationale at Paris, Fonds Français 2168, By the Care of F.W. Bourdillon. Oxford: Clarendon Press, 1896.

This, the only facsimile edition of *AN*, was consulted by several of the editors (notably Walther Suchier, Thomov, and Bourdillon himself) in lieu of the manuscript. The quasi-facsimile printing of the text (done with recourse to the manuscript) is a remarkable typographical achievement. Lengthy introduction includes a description of the manuscript and remarks on its graphic traits; notes cover reading problems.

B. SELECTED TRANSLATIONS

Aucassin et Nicolete has been translated at least forty times, into several modern European languages. The following list is intended to be representative rather than exhaustive. Besides the often-printed and widely-distributed versions of Andrew Lang (Bb4), Eugene Mason (Bb9), and Alexandre Bida (Ba5), it includes translations that are noteworthy because of their introductory or accompanying material, because of the translator's own importance, or by reason of their interest as bibliographical items. Arrangement is alphabetical by language (except that French, English and German are considered separately) and chronological for a given language.

For scholars and the reading public alike, throughout modern times, *Aucassin et Nicolete* has usually seemed to be a charming, escapist fantasy. Pre-Romantics, Romantics, Pre-Raphaelites and Symbolists alike saw in the text those elements of sentimentality and exoticism that were also part and parcel, in their way, of most scholarly accounts of the work given in the nineteenth and early twentieth centuries. The result, where translations of *AN* into the modern languages are concerned, is a marked tendency to occasional censoring of the medieval text, to artificial archaism in the translation, to lush sentimentalism in the illustrations, and to flights of fancy in the accompanying material. The work's reputation as a paean to youthful love has drawn to it both commercial publishers anxious to profit from its attractiveness by printing appealing translations, and translators (especially in English) whose qualifications for the rendering of a complex Old French text have often been embarrassingly short of the minimum required for simple accuracy.

The image of the work, then, long stimulated publication of illustrated editions for the general book trade. The fin-de-siècle translations of Lang and Henry, for example, are of greater interest for the history of popular culture than for the serious study of the *chantefable*, though we should not ignore their likely influence on the medievalists of our century, who may have been introduced to the text by way of these graceful but heavily ornamented renderings. Much the same may be said of the publication history of the translations. With the exception of those few scholarly or semi-scholarly versions better considered in conjunction with the editions they interpret (Dufournet, Thomov, Bourdillon and perhaps Bida) the works listed below are important mostly for the opportunity they offer to follow *AN* in its progress from the salons of the *genre-*

troubadour age into the parlours of Victorian Europe and America. An exception might be made for the important annotated version given by Wilhelm Hertz (Bc3, 1865), although Hertz never edited the work.

I have, then, made no systematic attempt to elucidate the often complex publication histories of translations such as Lang's, nor have I indicated, except in a few cases, some important features which are of interest primarily to descriptive bibliography.

Ba. MODERN FRENCH

Ba1. La Curne de Sainte-Palaye, Jean-Baptiste de. *Histoire ou romance d'Aucassin et de Nicolette. Mercure de France* (février 1752), 10-64. Rpt in *Les Amours du bon vieux temps.* Paris and Vaucluse: Duchesne, 1756, 1760. Revd version by Rémy de Gourmont. *C'est d'Aucasin et de Nicolete, Chantefable du XIIIe siècle.* Paris: L'Ymagier [1898]. Rpt of revd version. *C'est d'Aucasin et de Nicolete. Aucassin et Nicolette. Chantefable du XIIIe siècle.* Paris: Lutétia, 1936. (See Aa25.)

A very free adaptation, partly Bowdlerized; Torelore episode is included. Brief introduction.

Ba2. Legrand d'Aussy, Jean-Baptiste. *Fabliaux ou contes du XIIe et du XIIIe siècle, traduits ou extraits d'après divers manuscrits du tems.* 4 vols. Paris: E. Onfroy, for the Author, 1779-81. II, pp. 180-209. 2nd ed. 1781. III, pp. 30-72. 3rd ed., Paris: Renouard, 1829. III, pp. 341-73.

A very free prose rendering of Sainte-Palaye (Ba1). Cf. Aa3.

Ba3. *Histoire de la poésie provençale. Cours fait à la Faculté des Lettres de Paris par M.* [Claude] *Fauriel.* 3 vols. Paris: J. Labitte, 1846. III, pp. 180-218. 2nd ed. Leipzig: W. Engelmann, 1847.

Translates Méon's text (Aa1). Completed by Jules Mohl. Lacks Torelore episode. Fauriel assigns Provençal origin to *AN* (III, p. 183).

Ba4*. Delvau, Alfred. *Aucassin et Nicolette. Conte du XIIIe siècle.* In *Bibliothèque Bleue: Collection des Romans de Chevalerie.* Vol. III, no. 23. Paris: 1859, pp. 26-39. Rpt, under same title. 4 vols. Paris, 1859. I, pp. 314-27. 2nd ed. 1869. A revised version appears in *Aucassin et Nicolette. Roman de chevalerie...* publié avec introduction et traduction par A. Delvau. Paris: Bachelin-Deflorenne, 1866.

Inaccurate at best. See Aa6.

Ba5. *Aucassin et Nicolette.* Chantefable du douzième siècle.

Traduite par A[lexandre] Bida. Révision du texte original et préface par Gaston Paris. Paris: Hachette, 1878. Rpt Boston: Le Roy Phillips, n.d.
See also Aa7. Torelore episode omitted.

Ba6. *Aucassin et Nicolette. Chante-fable du XIIe siècle mise en français moderne par Gustave Michaut, avec une préface de Joseph Bédier.* Paris: Fontemoing [1901]. Revd eds 1905, 19??. Rpts Paris: Payot, 1917; Paris: Piazza, 1929; First ed. rpt Paris: E. de Boccard. 19??, 1947, 1964 (title page corrected to read "treizième siècle").
From Suchier's fourth ed. (Aa13); revd ed. from Suchier's fifth (Aa14). In the preface, Bédier speaks of *AN*'s "naïveté calculée," and compares the age of Watteau and Rameau; here, at the beginning of the thirteenth century, is a mixture of "[le] spontané" with "[le] factice." Introduction by Michaut.

Ba7. *Histoire d'Aucassin et de Nicolette.* Edited and Annotated by Ph. A. Guiton. London: Blackie and Son, 1921.
Not an edition, but a simplified adaptation intended for use as a school text.

Ba8. *Aucassin et Nicolette*, in *Les Contes du jongleur.* Trans. Albert Pauphilet. Paris: Piazza, 1932. Several rpts.
Pp. 93-172. See also the introduction, pp. v-viii. Based on Roques ed. (Aa24, 25).

Ba9*. *Aucassin et Nicolette.* Traduit du roman d'Oïl par Marcel Coulon. Nîmes: Calendal, 1933. Rpt with woodcuts by Valentin Le Campion. Uzès: Editions de la Cigale, 1936.

Ba10. *Aucassin et Nicolette and Four Lais of Marie de France*, Edited with Introduction, Notes and Vocabulary by Edwin B. Williams. New York: Crofts, 1933.
Modern French text for use in schools, abridged from Bida's (Ba5), with apparatus for classroom use. Once very widespread in the United States.

Ba11. *Aucassin et Nicolette. Chantefable du XIIIe siècle.* Traduction nouvelle en prose française moderne par Gustave Cohen. Paris: Champion, 1954. Rpt 1968, 1977.
From Roques ed. (Aa30, 1954 rpt).

Ba12*. *Aucassin et Nicolette*, chantefable du treizième siècle adaptée

par Maurice Pons. Paris: Pour les Impénitents [1960].
Illus. Edouard Pignon, Walther Spitzer.

Ba13. *Aucassin et Nicolette.* Trans. Jean Dufournet. Paris: Garnier-Flammarion, 1973.
See Aa41.

Bb. ENGLISH

Bb1*. *Tales of the Twelfth and Thirteenth Centuries.* 2 vols. 1786. II, pp. 125-60.

Bourdillon (Aa21) reports four other printings (1789, 1796, n.d., 1873, titles varying). From Legrand d'Aussy's prose adaptation. Legrand's version was also the source of Gregory Lewis Way's translation, in *Fabliaux or Tales.* 2 vols. London: W. Bulmer, 1796-1800. I, pp. 3-48. 2nd ed. 3 vols. London: Rodwell, 1815, with wood engravings by Bewick.

Bb2. *The Lovers of Provence. Aucassin and Nicolette.* A Ms. Song-Story of the Twelfth Century Rendered into Modern French by Alexandre Bida. Translated into English Verse and Prose by A. Rodney Macdonough. Illustrated with Engravings After Designs by A. Bida, Mary Hallock Foote, W.H. Gibson and F. Dielman. New York: Fords, Howard and Hulbert; New York: Dodge; Boston: Knight and Millet [all 1880].

Includes an English version of Gaston Paris's introduction (cf. Aa7).

Bb3. *Aucassin and Nicolette. A Love Story.* Edited in Old French and Rendered in Modern English (with Introduction, Glossary, Etc.) by F[rancis] W[illiam] Bourdillon. London: Kegan Paul, Trench and Co. 1887. 2nd revd ed. London and New York: Macmillan, 1897. The translation, slightly revised, appeared separately under the title *Aucassin and Nicolette.* Translated from the Old French by Francis William Bourdillon. London: Kegan Paul, Trench, Trübner and Co., 1903, rpt 1908.

It was further reprinted in London and Edinburgh: Foulis, 1908 (Cameron illustrations) and 1911 (Nash illus.); the 1908 ed. was reprinted in Philadelphia: G.W. Jacobs, 1909? (the ed. reported by LC under serial number NA 0489774 may tentatively be identified with this one) and the 1911 ed. was reprinted in Boston: LeRoy Phillips, 1913. Later Foulis eds. are dated 1913, 1920. Illustrations by Lettice Sandford accompany the ed. issued by the Folio Society in London, 1947.

With Lang (Bb4) and Mason (Bb9), the best-known English version. See also Aa10, Aa12 above, and cf. Benton L. Hatch, *A Check-List of the Publications of Thomas Bird Mosher* (Northampton: Univ. of Massachusetts Press, 1966), no. 445, perhaps a pirated rpt.

Bb4. *Aucassin and Nicolete.* Done Into English by Andrew Lang. London: David Nutt, 1887. 2nd ed. 1896, rpt 1898, 1904, 1910; New York: Stechert, 1928.

American ed. (pirated, according to Bourdillon and Suchier), Portland, Maine: Thomas B. Mosher, 1895 ("Old World Series", 2, 18 cm), rpt 1896, 1897, 1898 ("4th ed."), 1899 ("4th ed."), 1901, 1903, 1907, 1913, 1922, 1929; another rpt with Lang's name at head of title, 1903 ("The Vest Pocket Series", V, 14.5 cm), 1905, 1909. The 1889 Mosher ed. reported by LC is surely the 1899 rpt. See Benton L. Hatch, *A Check-List of the Publications of Thomas Bird Mosher* (Northampton: Univ. of Massachusetts Press, 1966), nos 12, 30, 53, 83, 126, 200, 266, 404, 596, 693; also 258, 346, 499.

Other eds: East Aurora, N.Y.: The Roycrofters, 1899; Chelsea: Ashendene Press, 1900; New Rochelle, N.Y.: Elston Press, 1902; London: Routledge; New York: Dutton, 1905 (other New York eds reported from Crowell; Base and Hopkins; and the Outing Press, all n.d.); Cincinnati: Fleuron Press, 1924; San Francisco: Windsor Press, 1926; New York: Limited Editions Club, 1931; New York: Holiday House, 1936; Mount Vernon, N.Y.: Golden Eagle Press, 1946; Lexington, Ky: Gravesend Press, 1957.

Lang's models include Bida (Ba5), Bourdillon (Bb3?). Brief introduction and notes.

Bb5*. *Aucassin and Nicholete. A Romance of the Twelfth Century.* Translated from the French by E[lias] J[ohn] W[ilkinson] Gibb. Glasgow, 1887.

Privately printed, in 50 copies, this translation also contains the text of Suchier's 2nd ed. (Aa9). Cf. Bourdillon, Aa12, p. xiii.

Bb6*. *This Is Of Aucasson and Nicolette. A Song-Tale of True Lovers.* Translated into English by M.S. Henry from the Little-Varying Old French Texts of H. Suchier, Gaston Paris, and F.W. Bourdillon, and the Verse Translation Rhymed by Edward W. Thomson. Boston: Copeland and Day, 1896. Rpt or reissue, 1897; Boston: Maynard, 1901 ("2nd ed."); Boston: Small, 1901; and under the title *Aucassin and Nicolette. An Old-French Song-Tale.* Translated by M.S. Henry. Versified by Edward W. Thomson. Edinburgh: O. Schulze [1902]. Rubricated. Rpt London:

Maclaren, n.d. (1905?).

As the latter ed. makes clear, Thomson is Henry's collaborator, not a model. R. Bossuat's 1256 is surely this translation (*Manuel bibliographique de la littérature française du moyen âge* (Melun: Librairie d'Argences, 1951)).

Bb7. *Nicolette and Aucassin. A Troubadour's Tale.* With a Critical and Biographical [sic] Introduction by Edward Everett Hale, Author of the Translation. New York: Appleton, 1899. Rpt 1901.

Most of the introduction is in fact an uninterrupted single direct quotation from Bourdillon's (Aa10).

Bb8. *Of Aucassin and Nicolette.* A Translation in Prose and Verse From the Old French, Together With *Amabel and Amoris.* Given for the First Time by Laurence Housman. With Drawings by Paul Woodroffe, Engraved on the Wood by Clemence Housman. London: J. Murray, [1902 or 1903]. Rpt London: Chatto and Windus; New York: Dial Press, 1925, 1930; Folcroft, Pa: Folcroft Library Eds, 1974; Norwood, Pa: Norwood Eds, 1977.

Amabel and Amoris is Housman's original composition, in imitation of *AN.*

Bb9. *Aucassin and Nicolette.* Translated from the Old French by Eugene Mason, with Coloured Plates by M[axwell] Armfield. London: Dent; New York: Dutton, 1910, rpt 1923. Rpt in *Aucassin and Nicolette and Other Medieval Romances and Legends.* Translated from the French by Eugene Mason. Everyman's Library, CDXCVII. London: Dent; New York: Dutton, 1910, 1912, 1915, 1919, 1928, 1937, 1942, 1951, etc. Also in *Old-World Love-Stories From the Lays of Marie de France, and Other Mediaeval Romances and Legends.* London: Dent; New York: Dutton, 1913. Illus. by Reginald Knowles.

Mason's models are Méon (Aa1) and Moland (Aa5).

Bb10. *Aucassin and Nicolete.* Done From the Old French by Michael West. Depictured by Main R. Bocher. Music by Horace Mansion. London: Harrap; New York: Brentano's [1917].

Coloured title page, coloured initials and borders; music for harp.

Bb11*. *Aucassin and Nicolette.* Translated by Edward Francis Moyer and Carey DeWitt Eldridge. Preface by Urban Tigner Holmes, Jr. Chapel Hill, N.C.: R[obert] Linker, 1937.

Cf. Aa32.

Bb12. *Aucassin and Nicolette.* In *The Ways of Love: Eleven Romances of Medieval France.* Trans. Norma Lorre Goodrich. New York: Beacon Press; Toronto: S.J. Reginald Saunders, 1964. Pp. 217-51.
Seems to have used both Roques (Aa30) and Suchier.

Bb13. *Aucassin and Nicolette and Other Tales.* Trans. Pauline Matarasso. Harmondsworth: Penguin Books, 1971. 160pp.
AN, pp. 15-57, 155-7. Brief introduction, limited notes. Uses Bourdillon (Aa12, 26), Suchier (Aa19) and Roques (Aa25, 36).

Bc. GERMAN

Bc1*. Wolff, Oskar Ludwig Bernhard. *Minerva: Taschenbuch für das Jahr 1833.* Leipzig, 1833. Pp. 117-64.
Based on Méon (Aa1). Rpt 1841.

Bc2*. Bülow, Eduard von. *Das Novellenbuch, oder Hundert Novellen nach alten Italienischen, Spanischen, Französischen* [etc.]. 4 vols. Leipzig: Brockhaus, 1834-6. III, pp. 30-9.
An adaptation of Sainte-Palaye (Ba1).

Bc3*. Hertz, Wilhelm. *Aucassin und Nicolette. Altfranzösischer Roman aus dem 13. Jahrhundert.* Vienna: K. Schönewerk, 1865. 2nd ed. Troppau: H. Kolck, 1868. Also in *Spielmannsbuch. Novellen in Versen aus dem 12n und 13n Jahrhundert.* Stuttgart: Kröner, then Cotta, 1886, 1900, 1905, 1912, 1931.
With scholarly notes (see Gaston Paris, *R*, XXIX (1900), 159, 292).

Bc4*. Gundlach, Fritz. *Aucassin und Nicolete. Ein altfranzösischer Roman aus dem 13. Jahrhundert.* Leipzig: Reclam [1890 or 1891].

Bc5*. Sallwürk, Edmund von. *Aucassin und Nicolette. Eine altfranzösische Novelle.* Frei Ubertragen von Edmund von Sallwürk. Leipzig: A.G. Liebeskind, 1896.

Bc6*. Schäfenacker, Paul. *Aucassin und Nicolete. Ein altfranzösischer Roman aus dem dreizehnten Jahrhundert.* Halle/Saale: Otto Hendel [1903].
With Introduction.

Bc7. Hansmann, Paul. In *Altfranzösische Novellen*, ed. Paul Ernst. 2 vols. Leipzig: Insel, 1909. I, pp. 114-211. Separate rpt under the title *Die Geschichte von Aucasin und Nicolete.* Leipzig: Insel [1912].

Bc8*. Oppeln-Bronikowski, Friedrich. *Aucassin und Nicolette. Altfranzösische Liebesmär.* Leipzig: C.F. Amelang, 1919.

Bc9*. Rieger, Erwin. *Aucassin und Nicolette.* Vienna: Avalun-Vertrag, 1919.
Woodcuts and other decoration by Rudolf Junk.

Bd. OTHER LANGUAGES

See also the lists given by Suchier, Aa19, pp. vii-viii; Bourdillon, Aa21, pp. 70-4.

Bd1. [*Bulgarian*] Thomov, Thomas S. *Aucassin et Nicolette. Chantefable du XIIIe siècle.* Sofia: Presses Universitaires, 1946.
See Aa34.

Bd2*. [*Czech*] Holk, Adolf. *Aucassin a Nicoletta.* Prague: J. Laichter, 1909.

Bd3*. [*Danish*] Michaëlis, Sophus. *Aucassin og Nicolete. En Oldfransk Kaerlighedsroman fra omtrent aar 1200.* Copenhagen: Reitzel [1893].

Bd4*. [*Dutch*] Decroos, J. *Aucassin en Nicolette.* Verhaal uit het Fransch der XIIIe Eeuw. Antwerp: De Sikkel [1930].

Bd5. [*Hebrew*] Goldberg, Leah.

וזה המעשה באוקאסן וניקולט. תרגמה מן המקור וציירה לאה גולדברג. ירושלים. ספרי תרשיש [1966]

Aucassin et Nicolette. Trans. and illus., Leah Goldberg. Jerusalem and Tel-Aviv: Tarshish Books, Dvir, 1966.

Bd6*. [*Hungarian*] Arpád, Tóth. *Aucasin es Nicolete. Ofrancia széphistoria.* Gyoma: Knew̋ Isidor könyvnyomtato, 1921.

Bd7*. [*Italian*] Boselli, Antonio. *Aucassin e Nicoletta.* Saggio de traduzione dall'antico francese per cura di Antonio Boselli. Bologna, 1906. Rpt under the title *Aucassin e Nicoletta, Cantafavola francese del secolo XII*, per la prima volta tradutta in italiano da Antonio Boselli. Parma: Battei, 1906.
The versions given by Luigi Orsini, *Con l'amore e con l'ala. L'aurea legenda dugentesca di Alcassino e Nicoletta*, rinnovellata da Luigi Orsini. Milan: Hoepli, [1922?], and Carlo Raimondo, *Alcassino e Nicoletta. Fiaba drammatica in quattro atti* (Milan: [Bottega di poesia], 1923), appear to be adaptations rather than translations.

Bd8*. [*Polish*] Roques reports (Aa30, p. *d*) a translation by Wl. Kopaczynski (Leopol, 1914).

Bd9*. [*Russian*] Liverovskaïa. G. Lozinski (*R*, L (1924), 318) reports a translation "publiée par Mme Liverovskaïa dans la revue 'Rousskaïa Mysl' (mars 1914, pp. 167-204)". Roques (Aa30, p. *d*) reports another translation by A.A. Smirnov (Moscow, 1935).

Bd10*. [*Serbo-Croatian*] Leskovac, Mladen. *Povest o Okaseny i Nikoleti.* Novi Sad: Matica Srpska, 1965.

Bd11*. [*Swedish*] Feilitzen, Hugo von. *Aucassin och Nicolett. Fornfransk Fableau. Ny Svensk Tidskrift* (1889), 368-400.

Be. DRAMATIC ADAPTATIONS

The theatrical aspect of *AN* has inspired more than one stage version of the work, the first probably having been Jean-Michel Sedaine's *Aucassin et Nicolette ou les Moeurs du bon vieux temps*, with music by Grétry (1779). This adaptation, and the "parodie en trois actes" entitled *Marcassin et Tourlourette* (1780), bear witness to the popularity of La Curne de Sainte-Palaye's version (Ba1). See also the list of comedies, parodies, mimes, operas and the like in Suchier (Aa23), pp. x-xi (and cf. Bourdillon's various bibliographies). To that list should be added the adaptations by L'Hôpital and Sauvageot (1939: "rédigé spécialement en vue d'être mimé par des enfants de 8 à 18 ans"); Pierre Sadron and René Clermont (1947?) and others. Note especially the "action musicale" by G. Massias, reported by Dufournet, Aa41, p. 34: *Les Nouveaux racontars d'Agassin et Virelette*, "parodie d'une parodie, servie par des acteurs-musiciens, unissant l'ancien français à l'argot moderne, les cromornes, les flûtes à bec et les bombardes aux techniques les plus audacieuses de la musique moderne", and also the videotape of a 1974 performance done under the direction of Raymond J. Cormier of Temple University (1954 Cohen translation, see above, Ba11) and distributed by the International Courtly Literature Society.

CRITICAL STUDIES

by

Barbara Nelson Sargent-Baur

C. CRITICAL STUDIES

References to line numbers in the prose sections of *AN* are to the numbering used in the Roques edition (Aa24, etc.).

1873

1 Pater, Walter. *Studies in the History of the Renaissance.* London: Macmillan, 1873.

Pp. 1-17 contain a study of *AN*, based on Fauriel's 1846 translation (Ba3). This is the response of an aesthetic critic to the text. Pater concentrates on those elements that produce "pleasurable sensations", especially the descriptive details. He finds therein a "languid Eastern deliciousness". Also attractive to him is the spirit of intellectual independence and rebellion that he believes the Hell-Paradise speech expresses.

1877

2 Pater, Walter. *The Renaissance: Studies in Art and Poetry.* London: Macmillan, 1877, 1888, 1897, etc.

A revd ed. of C1. The material on *AN* (pp. 1-30) lacks Fauriel's translation of the Hell-Paradise speech, included in the *Studies* chapter.

1878

3 Mussafia, A. "Cateron." *ZRP*, III (1878), 267.

Derives *cateron* (*AN* XIV, 20) from *caput* with diminutive suffix *-er -on.*

1879

4 Paris, Gaston. (Untitled) review of Suchier[1], Paris/Bida et al., in *R*, VIII (1879), 284-93.

Much of this is an appreciation of Suchier's 1878 edition (Aa8), drawing attention to its accuracy, erudition, and rich critical apparatus. Considerable comparison with Paris's own 1878 edition (Aa7), and some with Méon's (Aa1). Comments on Tobler's review (Aa8.4) of Suchier[1]. Discusses the use of accents, and certain meanings; proposes 12th-century composition and a single author. A detailed and careful contribution, fair even in disagreement.

1880

5 Brunner, Hugo. *Über Aucassin und Nicolete.* Halle, 1880. 32pp.

This Inaugural Dissertation (Halle/Wittenberg), republished in 1881 in a program of the Realschule of Kassel, compares *AN* with *Floire et Blancheflor* and postulates an earlier redaction of *FB* than has come down to us as a source of *AN.* Contains a useful bibliography of editions, translations, and adaptations.

Review: .1 J. Koch, *LGRP* (7 July, 1881), col. 248.

1882

6* Schlickum, Julius. "Die Wortstellung in der altfranzösischen Dichtung *Aucassin et Nicolete.*" In *Französische Studien.* Ed. G. Körting and E. Koschwitz. Heilbronn: Henninger, 1882, III, 3, pp. 177-222.

1889

7 Lang, Andrew. *Letters on Literature.* London: Longmans, Green, 1889, 1892, 1893, 1896.

On pp. 80-91, a "Letter" on *AN*, a reworking of the Introduction to Lang's translation (Bb4). It consists mainly of a short, chatty, popular retelling of the plot.

8 Suchier, Hermann. "Zu *Aucassin* (tateron, soïsté)." *ZRP*, XIV (1889), 175.

Proposes correcting the *cateron* of XIV, 20, to *tateron<tetta.* Considers *soïsté* (<*societatem*) of IV, 24, as trisyllabic.

1892

9 Thurneysen, Rudolf. "Zur Stellung des Verbums in Altfranzösischen." *ZRP*, XVI (1892), 289-307.

Draws on the prose passages of *AN* to show that the position of the verb in the sentence is not haphazard but subject to rules that regularly apply.

1900

10 Paris, Gaston. *Poèmes et légendes du moyen âge.* Paris: Société d'Edition Artistique, 1900.

A slightly abridged reprinting of the Preface to Paris's 1878 edition (Aa7) is on pp. 97-112. Paris stresses the oral character of the work, intended not to be read so much as recited, "presque jouée".

11 Paris, Gaston. (Untitled) review, in *R*, XXIX (1900), 287-92.

This is for the most part a review of reviews, though it also appraises Sucher[4] (Aa13) and Bourdillon (Aa12, Ab1). It treats Schulze's reviews of Suchier[3] and Suchier[4] (Aa11.1, Aa13.2) and Tobler's review of Suchier[1] (Aa8.4), and Brunner's dissertation (C5). Paris has been persuaded by Suchier that *AN* comes not from Champagne but from Artois. He remains convinced of the inferiority of the second part.

1904

12 Adams, Henry. *Mont-Saint-Michel and Chartres.* Washington, 1904; Boston: Houghton, Mifflin, 1905, etc.

Ch. XII, entitled "Nicolette and Marion", gives about a dozen pages (depending on the edition) to *AN.* The discussion is based on the 1898 facsimile published by Bourdillon (Ab1), with *antif* of I, 2, corrected to *caitif.* Adams takes the *cantefable* as the product of a poet-troubadour, perhaps a crusader with Richard Lionheart and Philippe Auguste. It is, for him, an exquisite expression of courteous love. The analysis, illustrated by lengthy excerpts and translations (presumably by Adams) ends with the reunion of the lovers, who ride off together. This truncated presentation supports Adams's view that *AN*, like nearly all the medieval romances, is "singularly pure and refined".

13 Crescini, Vincenzo. *Dai tempi antichi ai tempi moderni.* Milan, 1904.

On pp. 49-50, comment on XV, 18 (retains MS reading). See C15.

14 Foerster, Wendelin. "Randglossen zur Cantefable." *ZRP*, XXVIII (1904), 492-512.

Contains detailed commentary on Suchier[5] (Aa14). Agrees with many of Suchier's readings and corrections, and proposes some new ones. Advocates a systematic use of diacritical marks to show Picard pronunciations. As to the author, region, and date, Foerster finds echoes of Chrétien de Troyes (*Erec*, *Charrete*, *Graal*) and postulates a parodic intent and much originality; this is not the work of a *Spielmann.* Proposes a date after the *Graal* but before 1200 (acknowledging that the question is delicate) and an origin in the Walloon region (i.e., the Northeast, rather than Suchier's North). The study concentrates, most learnedly, on paleography, phonology, and dialectology.

1906

15 Suchier, Hermann. "Zu *Aucassin und Nicolette.*" *ZRP*, XXX (1906), 513-21.

An answer to C14, taking the points in order and generally reasserting his original positions. Also discusses Crescini (C13).

1908

16 Piccoli, Raffaello, "L'assonanza dei *vers orphelins* in *Aucassin et Nicolette.*" *ZRP*, XXXII (1908), 600-3.

Discusses the "corrections" made by Suchier in his editions (Aa8, 9, 11, 13, 14, 16) so as to make the final line of each *laisse* assonate in *i*. Piccoli argues tellingly against these changes.

1909

17 Blondheim, D.S. "A Parallel to *Aucassin et Nicolette*, VI, 26." *MLN*, XXIV (1909), 73-4.
Finds a parallel to Aucassin's Hell-Paradise speech in a tale about Machiavelli, quoted by Pierre Bayle in his *Dictionnaire historique et critique*. Marginal.

1910

18 Acher, Jean. "Remarques sur le texte d'*Aucassin et Nicolette.*" *ZRP*, XXXIV (1910), 369-73.
Commentary on III, 5; VI, 21f, 51, 59; XV, 1, 17; XVI, 17; conjecture about the "borrowed" melodies.

19 Meyer-Lübke, Wilhelm. "*Aucassin und Nicolette.*" *ZRP*, XXXIV (1910), 513-22.
Concentrates on the dramatic aspect of *AN*, which differentiates it from other works (e.g., Arabic or Irish) that alternate prose and verse. Attributions of spoken lines and indications of movement are analogous to stage-directions; the repeated formulae "or se cante", "or dient..." were probably intended for the several actors. Postulates the creation of *AN* around Arras, at the end of the 12th or beginning of the 13th century, corresponding with the development of the theater there. An important study, though the dating is questionable.

20 Söderhjelm, Werner. *La Nouvelle française au XVe siècle.* Paris: Champion, 1910.
Discusses, pp. 8-15, *AN* among examples of the *nouvelle* before the 15th century. Considers it as a transitional stage between verse and prose narrative, the verse sections tending toward description and the expression of feeling, the prose passages toward action. Praises the lack of sentimentality and the new vivacity and naturalness of the prose; criticizes the concession to the contemporary taste for oriental adventures. A judicious and perceptive, though brief, analysis.

1911

21 Aschner, S. "Zu *Aucassin und Nicolette.*" *ZRP*, XXXV (1911), 741-3.
Argues that *AN* is a mime, rather than a dramatic work, as Meyer-Lübke claimed (in C19).

22 Beck, J.B. "La Musique des chansons de geste". In *Comptes*

Rendus des Séances de l'Académie des Inscriptions et Belles Lettres (1911), pp. 39-45.
Discusses the *vers récitatif* with four stresses and the *vers orphelin.* The music accompanying the *laisses* of *AN* comes up for comment.

23 Brandin, Louis. "*Aucassin et Nicolette*, XXI, 5-8." *MLR*, VI (1911), 100-3.
The MS gives the hypermetric reading "cors corset". Brandin would eliminate "cors" and interpret "corset" as "petit corps, taille fine". (Most critics now take it as designating part or all of a garment.)

24 Johnston, O.M. "Origin of the Legend of *Floire and Blancheflor.*" In *Matzke Memorial Volume, Containing Two Unpublished Papers by John E. Matzke and Contributions in his Memory by his Colleagues.* Leland Stanford Junior University Publications, University Series. Stanford: University Press, 1911, pp. 125-38.
Pp. 129-34 present similarities between *AN* and *FB.*

1912

25 Crescini, Vincenzo. "Per l'esordio della cantafavola su *Alcassino e Nicoletta.*" In *Studi dedicati a Francesco Torraca nel XXXVI anniversario della sua laurea.* Naples: Perella, 1912, pp. 381-7.
Concentrates on I, 2, and proposes to read *deport* not as *diletto* but as *portamento, condotta.* Hence this verse would mean "of the behaviour of the very old man (i.e., Aucassin's father)". The examples in Godefroy, cited in support, are either late or ambiguous.

26 Lot-Borodine, Myrrha. *Le Roman idyllique au moyen âge.* Paris, 1912; rpt Geneva: Slatkine, 1972.
Gives a whole chapter (pp. 75-134) to *AN.* Draws attention to the objectivity and delicate irony of the author, which contrast sharply with the tone of *Floire et Blancheflor* (analysed in Ch. I). A perceptive study of the artistry of *AN.*

27 Thurau, Gustav. *Singen und sagen: ein Beitrag zur Geschichte des dichterischen Ausdrucks.* Berlin: Weidmann, 1912.
Takes up *AN* on pp. 76-84 in a judicious study of the relationship between the verse and prose sections. Proposes that the use of assonated *laisses* is not necessarily a sign of a very early composition; it may well be a deliberate archaism.
Review: .1 J.B. Beck, *ZFSL*, XLI, 2 (1913), 136-66.

1913

28 Dockhorn, Rudolf. *Zur Textkritik von 'Aucassin und Nicolette.'*

Halle: Hohmann, 1913, 90pp.
The first part discusses in much detail the divergent readings appearing in the editions, and the corrections proposed both in these editions and in critical articles. The second part suggests further corrections and attempts to explain difficult passages; its tendency is to unify the text.

29 Faral, Edmond. *Recherches sur les sources latines des contes et romans courtois du moyen âge.* Paris: Champion, 1913.
Makes a careful comparison (pp. 26-33) of situations and themes in *AN* and *Piramus et Tisbé*, and suggests the latter as one source of the former.

1914

30 Heiss, Hanns. "Die Form der Cantefable." *ZFSL*, XLII (1914), 250-62.
Thinks, incorrectly, that *AN*'s mixture of prose and verse is original. Disagrees with Meyer-Lübke (C19) on the function of certain indications of movement in the text.

31 Suchier, Walther. "Das Problem des französischen Verses." *ZFSL*, XLII (1914), 208-50.
Gives some pages (221-3, 240-1) to a study of the first eleven *laisses*, in an attempt to determine which syllable in the line is most often accentuated. Arrives at some very definite conclusions, without sufficiently taking into account the music that accompanies the verse and that has its own stresses.

1918

32 Settegast, F. "Die Odyssee oder die Sage des heimkehrenden Gatten als Quelle mitteralterliches Dichtung." *ZRP*, XXXIX (1918), 266-329.
Pp. 282-90 offer some freewheeling speculation on characters and places in Homer as prototypes of those in *AN*.

1922

33 Scheludko, D[mitri]. "Zur Entstehungsgeschichte von *Aucassin et Nicolete*." *ZRP*, XLII (1922), 458-90.
Considers and rejects the theory of oriental sources for *AN*, on the grounds that many of the situations and episodes are commonplaces of French medieval literature and of folk-tale, and that Arabic names were easy to come by. Believes that *AN* and *Floire et Blanchefleur* are independent of each other. A sensible, erudite article.
Review: .1 L. Jordan (see C34).

1924

34 Jordan, Leo. "Die Quellen des *Aucassins* und die Methode des Urteils in der Philologie." *ZRP*, XLIV (1924), 291-307.

Starts from the conflicting views of Scheludko (C33) on medieval European sources, and of W. Suchier (Aa22) on Oriental sources. He finds the latter more probable, and opts specifically for a tale in *One Thousand and One Nights*, that of "Ward and Prince Uns". His arguments are interesting but not conclusive. He is severe toward other scholars whom he thinks either doctrinaire or subjective, especially Lerch (Aa22.1, 27.1), to whom he erroneously attributes the Romantic notion of the "Dichter ein Schöpfer". The article claims to be an exposition of sound methodology; it does not answer to its ambitious title. See C40.

1925

35 Krappe, Alexander H. "Two Ancient Parallels to *Aucassin et Nicolette*,VI, 34-40." *Philological Quarterly*, IV (1925), 180-1.

Sees similarities between the inhabitants of Paradise according to Aucassin and the categories of people found by Aeneas at the Styx in the *Aeneid*, VL. The reference to the "beles dames cortoises" recalls Seneca's strictures against adultery in *De Beneficiis.* Virgil and Seneca being well known in the Middle Ages, Krappe thinks they may have inspired the author of *AN.* If so, then the prose-verse alternation may be due not to Oriental influence but to Boethius. More speculative than enlightening.

36 Roques, Mario. "Pour le commentaire d'*Aucassin et Nicolette*, 'esclairier le cuer'." In *Mélanges d'histoire du moyen âge offerts à M. Ferdinand Lot par ses amis et ses élèves.* Paris: Champion, 1925, pp. 723-36.

Commentary on III, 13-18, and specifically on 16, corrected by all editors since Suchier to read *m'esclaire* (MS: *mel craire*). Roques retains and justifies the gloss in his 1925 edition (Aa24), offering 26 examples taken from other OF texts: it signifies *soulager, ôter le coeur de peine, d'inquiétude.* The worry involved is Aucassin's concerning Nicolete's birth and hence worthiness to be his wife. To his mother, who has just exhorted him to forget N. and marry a girl of good family, A. replies (1.13) "mere, je n'en puis el faire", I cannot do otherwise than you say if I marry Nicolete. (She is well-born, "de boin aire", 1.14, distinguished and beautiful; I have no worries on the score of her birth.) An example of philology at its best. See also C69.

Review: .1 M. Roques, *R*, LII (1926), 369.

(Gives a summary of the above article and adds one more example, from the *Siège de Barbastre.*)

37 Reinhard, John R. "The Literary Background of the *Chantefable*." *Speculum*, I (1926), 157-69.
Examines the literary antecedents of the alternate prose and verse of *AN*. Although there are analogues in Arabic, Celtic, and Old Norse literature, the usual practice of French medieval authors was to look for literary guides in the traditions of classical antiquity. Examples begin with Menippus and include Varro, Seneca, Petronius, and Apuleius; Reinhard follows the device through Martianus Capella, Dante, Boccaccio, and Sidney, to the *Satire Ménippée* of 1593. In short, the *prosimetrum* style is employed in a considerable body of literature. A learned and clearly-written article.

1927

38 Foulet, Lucien. "'Si m'ait Dieus' et l'ordre des mots." *R*, LIII (1927), 301-24.
Studies the nature of the *si-se* in the ancient formula (used four times in *AN*) to try to ascertain whether the initial word is an adverb or a conjunction; this has implications for word order. A penetrating and meticulous article.

39 Suchier, Walther. "Weiteres zu *Aucassin und Nicolette*." In *Philologische Studien aus dem romanisch-germanischen Kulturkreise Karl Voretzsch dargebracht.* Ed. B. Schädel and W. Mulertt. Halle: Niemeyer, 1927, pp. 155-72.
Examines proper names and literary themes in *AN* and submits that they are suggestive of Arabic influence. Presents the views of a number of other scholars on this. The study shows commendable caution and balance.

1928

40 Scheludko, D[mitri]. "Orientalisches in der altfranzösischen erzählenden Dichtung." *ZFSL*, LI (1928), 255-93.
Takes up a number of motifs appearing in OF literature and attributed by some (e.g. Jordan, C34) to Oriental origins. Shows that these are international commonplaces; it is idle to search for specific sources. Discusses *AN* among other works as reflecting a widespread medieval taste for exotic names and places. An article remarkable for its learning and reasonableness. See C85.

1929

41 Krappe, Alexander H. "Sur une forme noroise d'un épisode d'*Aucassin et Nicolette*." *R*, LV (1929), 260-3.
The episode is that in which the fugitive Nicolete asks some shepherds to tell Aucassin of a wonderful "beast" (i.e. herself) to be hunted in the

forest. In the *Thidreks Saga*, a neglected wife tells her husband to hunt a "beast" (the traces of which she herself has left in the snow with her body), or else someone else may catch it. This story may be based on a hellenistic tale in Parthenius: a neglected wife follows her husband on a hunt and spies on him in disguise; her husband's dogs find her and tear her apart. The resemblances among these three tales seem rather slight, although Krappe finds them striking. He raises but does not answer the question of Oriental influence on *AN*.

1930

42 Storost, W. *Geschichte des altfranzösischen und altprovenzalischen Romanzenstrophe.* Romanistische Arbeiten, XVI. Halle, 1930.
Gives three pages (56-8) to an analysis of the melodies accompanying the verse sections.

43 Velten, Harry V. "Le Conte de la *fille biche* dans le folklore français." *R*, LVI (1930), 282-8.
Considers that Nicolete's cryptic message to Aucassin, entrusted to the shepherds, to come hunt a valuable beast in the woods is an allusion to the popular tale of a girl transformed into a doe. Gives parallels in French and other literatures. Possible, but not conclusive.

1931

44 Neri, F. "Viel antif." *Atti della (Reale) Academia delle Scienze di Torino*, LXVI (1931), 195-8.
Viel antif may be read as an adjectival phrase modifying *deport*; it would thus mean "of days gone by, of once upon a time". There is nothing inherently impossible in this interpretation.
Review: .1 M. Roques (see C48).

45 Tanquerey, F.J. "Imprécations comminatoires en ancien français (à propos d'un passage d'*Aucassin et Nicolette*)." *R*, LVII (1931), 562-8.
Interprets *AN* II, 23, and VIII, 20 ("Ja Dix ne me doinst riens que je li demant...") as a temporal construction: "Que Dieu soit sourd à mes prières, quand je serai chevalier et que je monterai à cheval pour aller au combat...si vous me refusez Nicolette." This, though, makes little sense in the context of Aucassin's refusal to engage in knightly activities. Tanquerey proposes to change *ne monte a ceval* to *se monte a ceval.* This seems arbitrary, especially since *ne monte* occurs twice and is probably not a scribal error. The interpretation advanced is questionable. Answered by Roques, C50.

1932

46 Frank, Grace. "The Cues in *Aucassin et Nicolette*." *MLN*, XLVII

(1932), 14-16.
The formulae "or se cante" and "or dient et content et fabloient" appear to be cues. The arrangement of the lines and the large red initials in the MS make it clear that "or se cante" was, for the scribe, to be attached to the ends of the prose portions and "or dient..." to the ends of the parts in verse. Starting with the end of the first passage, each subsequent section was introduced by a cue, reciter to singer, singer to reciter. It would follow that *AN* was destined for performance by two persons. A careful and well-argued study.
Review: .1 M. Roques (see C48).
(Agrees that the formulae "or se cante" and "or dient..." are not titles, and thinks he erred in arranging them as such in his edition (Aa24, 25). Is unconvinced that they represent spoken cues, holding them to be stage-directions.)

47 Gérold, Théodore. *La Musique au moyen âge.* CFMA, LXXIII. Paris: Champion, 1932.
A standard work. Ch. IX, "La Musique des chansons de geste", gives several pages to *AN*, particularly the problems posed by the numerous *laisses* containing an odd number of long lines. Postulates that the performer had sometimes to repeat the second musical phrase. Musically, *AN* offers more variety than the monotonous, one-phrase *chanson de geste.*

48 Roques, Mario. "Notes diverses sur *Aucassin et Nicolette.*" *R*, LVI (1932), 447-50.
Discusses Neri (C44), Frank (C46), and Williams (C49).

49 Williams, J. Killa. "A Disputed Reading in *Aucassin et Nicolette*, I, 2." *MLR*, XXVII (1932), 62-3.
A very slight note, heavy in speculation and light in documentation, rehearsing a number of old hypotheses concerning *viel antif* and opting for *caitif*, one sign among many that the author may have been a foreigner and perhaps an Arab.
Review: .1 M. Roques (see C48).

1933

50 Roques, Mario. "Sur deux leçons contestées du manuscrit d'*Aucassin et Nicolette.*" In *Mélanges de philologie offerts à Jean-Jacques Salverda de Grave.* Groningen and The Hague: J.B. Wolters, 1933; rpt Geneva: Slatkine, 1972, pp. 263-71.
Mainly a reply to Tanquerey (C45), rejecting his interpretation of *quant* in "quant ere cevaliers" (II, 23, and VIII, 20) as temporal. For Roques it is hypothetical: "Que Dieu ne m'accorde plus rien, si jamais je suis

chevalier et que je monte à cheval...si vous ne me donnez Nicolette." Finds an analogy in X, 52-3. As for the difficult V, 60, R. gives a summary of the solutions proposed by different editors, himself included, and now corrects Suchier's reading (followed by R. in Aa24 and 25). *Aioire* is an interrogative exclamation. The line should read: " 'Sire, voire fait! Aioire?' fait li quens." This is most persuasive.

51 Roques, Mario. "Pour le commentaire d'*Aucassin et Nicolette.*" *R*, LIX (1933), 423-31.
A development of C50. *Ai oire* (X, 60) is probably equivalent to "allons" or "eh! bien!"

1934

52 Sauter, Hermann. *Wortgut und Dichtung. Eine lexicographisch-literaturgeschichtliche Studie über den Verfasser des altfranzösischen Cantefable 'Aucassin et Nicolette'.* Arbeiten zur Romanischen Philologie, hgg. von E. Lerch, XIV. Münster: Selbstverlag des Romanischen Seminars, 1934. xxii + 208pp.
A lexicographical and stylistic study, stressing the author's taste for colorful, concrete, expressive language. Tries, not very convincingly, to reconstruct the author's personality and place of origin. Some of the inferences from the choice of words are rather dubious.
Reviews: .1 J. Orr, *MLR*, XXXI (1936), 96-100.
(Concludes with commentary on XXI, 8 [*cors corset*], V, 14 [*a miramie*], and XIV, 20 [*cateron*].)
.2 M. Roques, *R*, LXIII (1936), 404-5.
(Carries the puzzling annotation "Munster, et Paris, Droz, 1934".)

53 Vendryès, J. "La Couvade chez les Scythes." *Académie des Inscriptions et Belles-Lettres. Comptes rendus des séances de l'année 1934*, 329-39.
Treats the custom as reported by Herodotus and Hippocrates and as observed here and there in the 20th century. It shows up in ancient Irish literature. Properly, the *couvade* involved the father's taking care of the new-born child and staying in bed or at least indoors, while the mother provided food and did outside work. No specific mention of *AN*, but interesting and informative.

1934-5

54 Chatelain, Y. "A propos d'Aucassin et Nicolette." *Les Humanités*, XI (1934-5), 285-8.
Considers, on insufficient grounds (the insolence of the ox-driver and the shepherds) that the author knew the Midi.

1935

55 Roques, Mario. "Ancien français *ai oire, ai or, aaire, ore ai.*" *R*, LXI (1935), 360-2.

Gives two more examples from other works of the expression *ai oire* occurring in *AN*, X, 60.

1936

56 Gérold, Théodore. *Histoire de la musique des origines à la fin du XIVe siècle.* Paris: Renouard, 1936.

Brief mention (pp. 262-3) of the melodies of *AN*; the fact that some of the *laisses* have an odd number of long lines implies a repetition of one of the long musical phrases. *AN* is not listed in the index (which gives only the names of composers), and the discussion of its music is buried in a chapter on "la musique profane des IXe, Xe et XIe siècles".

57 Levy, Raphael. "The Old-French Interjection *aioire.*" *MLR*, XXXI (1936), 65-8.

Agrees with Roques's transcription of *AN*, X, 60, *aioire*. Proposes emending X, 59, "ie vos ai pris" to read "ie nes ai pris" (=les armes), i.e. "Have I not taken them up?" The correction seems uncalled-for.

58 Urwin, Kenneth. "The Setting of *Aucassin et Nicolette.*" *MLR*, XXXI (1936), 403-5.

Shows that some of the geographical details in Beaucaire as they appear in *AN* are more realistic than had been thought (e.g. that the city probably was accessible from the sea in the Middle Ages). A misunderstanding of the meaning of *castel* leads Urwin to suppose that the battle waged by Count Bougars takes place in the streets of the town.

1937

59 Schulze, Alfred. "Zum *Aucassin.*" *ZFSL*, LXI (1937), 205-10.

Interprets the first word, *qui*, as interrogative, and the whole first sentence as an invitation. The *viel antif* of 1. 2 is the author, who takes pleasure (*deport*) in the adventures of A. and N. In XIV, 5 ("ne qui vos porroit"), *porroit* is a transitive verb: "or who would have power over you". These interpretations are reasonable.

1940

60 Reese, Gustave. *Music in the Middle Ages.* New York: Norton, 1940.

Brief mentions of the music for the verse portions and of the musical instruments named in *AN*, on pp. 204-5 and 328-9.

61 Schultz-Gora, Otto. "Afrz. *par que* (*coi*)." *ZRP*, LX (1940), 29-36.

On p. 33, discusses the expression as it appears in *AN*, XIV, 31, used by the watchman in the tower. Proposes the meaning "in der Weise dass", which seems plausible.

1941

62 Winkler, E. "Or dient et content et fabloient." *ZFSL*, LXIV, 5 (1941), 284-302; rpt in *Der altfranzösische höfische Roman.* Ed. Erich Köhler. Wege der Forschung, CDXXV. Darmstadt: Wissenschaftliche Buchgesellschaft, 1978, pp. 267-88.
Treats a variety of topics: scholars' debates (some of these rather dated), the relative importance of speech and song (thinks the verse sections take priority, the prose being largely mere connecting material), the complex *dient-content-fablent* (with nuances of these words), the label *cantefable* (*chante-fable*, a compound analogous to *garde-robe, porte-clef,* etc.). Interesting insights.

1942-3

63 Bar, Francis. "Sur un épisode d'*Aucassin et Nicolette*." *R*, LXVII (1942-3), 369-70.
Acknowledges the similarities noted by Roques (Aa25) between the traditional warning of the friendly sentinel to the lovers in the *chansons d'aube* and the watchman's advice to Nicolete. Proposes a second source of inspiration in the Song of Songs, where the Bride, in search of her beloved, complains of ill-treatment at the hands of the *custodes* (who found her, beat her, wounded her, and took away her cloak). Since in fact none of this happens in *AN*, the proposed source is dubious, to say the least.

1947-8

64 Spitzer, Leo. "Le vers 2 d'*Aucassin et Nicolette* et le sens de la chantefable." *MP*, XLV (1947-8), 8-14; rpt in *Romanische Literaturstudien 1936-1956.* Tübingen: Niemeyer, 1959, pp. 49-63.
Reads *deport* in 1. 2 as *conduite, attitude*, by analogy with English "deportment", and identifies the *viel antif* as Aucassin's father. The whole first sentence is made up of parallel prepositional phrases relating to *bons vers* of 1. 1 and beginning with *de.* It establishes a contrast between the old man's behaviour and that of two youngsters, thus underscoring the meaning of the tale: the clash of generations. Unfortunately, this use of *deport* in the sense of "behaviour" is not attested till the fifteenth century, and even then in English. (Mentions also the possibility of *mel* for *viel*, a reading suggested by Stengel in Aa8.3, p. 152 and reported by W. Suchier in Aa22, p. 35.) See C67, 74.

1948

65 Chailley, Jacques. "Etudes musicales sur la chanson de geste." *Revue de Musicologie*, XXIX (1948), 3-4.

Proposes that the coupling of musical phrases with the verses of the *laisses* be done not by a mechanical alternation ABAB but according to the sense and syntax of the lines. A sensible suggestion.

1949

66 Cohen, Gustave. "Une curieuse et vieille coutume folklorique: la couvade (la femme accouche et l'homme se couche)."*Psyché*, IV (1949), 80-92; *Symposium*, III (1949), 214-35.

The same article, published twice; it lists some possible literary sources of the theme (in Plutarch, Herodotus, *et al.*). The custom was known in the Basque country, the Balearic Islands, and Sardinia; *AN*'s author, if cultivating Mediterranean local colour, might have used it on that account. On the other hand, there might be a Northern influence (in keeping with the Picard dialect of *AN*); the custom still existed in parts of Holland up to World War I. But the custom is widely dispersed, and symbolises (Cohen thinks) the androgynous nature of humanity. A diffuse, speculative study.

67 Frank, Grace. "*Aucassin et Nicolette*, 1. 2." *RR*, XL (1949), 161-4.

A reply to Spitzer (C64). In 1. 2 the penultimate word (*viel*?) is unclear; the three initial strokes may indicate *m* rather than *vi*. *Mel* (a graphy for *mal*), though not occurring elsewhere in *AN*, does turn up in other MSS of the 13th century and may well have been known to the scribe of *AN*. The *mel antif* would mean something like "the suffering of long ago" and form a contrast with *deport*; the pair of substantives would balance that in 11. 5-6, "des grans paines...et des proueces". L. 2 should read "del deport, du mel antif". This reading is plausible. See C74.

68 Levy, Raphael. "L'Emploi du mot *desport* (sic) dans *Aucassin et Nicolette*." *MLN*, LXIV (1949), 164-6.

Proposes that *viel antif* (1. 2) is a "surnom à deux éléments". It refers not to the author or to the *jongleur*, but to one of the characters: Aucassin's father. As for *deport*, Levy gives some ambiguous medieval passages using it and cites texts from the 16th and 17th centuries using *deportement* as equivalent to *conduite.* That such evidence substantiates his interpretation of *deport* in *AN* is less than certain.

69 Roques, Mario. " 'Sa biautés le cuer m'esclaire.' " In his *Etudes de*

littérature française. Lille: Giard; Geneva: Droz, 1949, pp. 43-52.
Rpt of C36.

1950

70 Pauphilet, Albert. *Le Legs du moyen âge.* Bibliothèque Elzévirienne, Nouvelle Série, Etudes et Documents. Melun: Librairie d'Argences, 1950.
All of the last chapter (pp. 239-48) is given to *AN*. Pauphilet considers this to be the product of a somewhat paradoxical mind; yet it is "une histoire d'amour fort simple". Complications found in it by earlier critics were their own creations. P. does note the parody: of courtesy and the themes of war and adventure. The most prominent technique is "une sorte de jeu permanent de contre-pied" of several kinds. Yet not all the situations and characters are ridiculous. The conclusion is that the author, while making fun of literary traditions, did not make them all equally laughable, and that he preserved a light touch. A perceptive study, in spite of some minor errors of detail.

71 Sansone, Giuseppe E. *Idillio e ironia in 'Aucassin e Nicolette.'* Bari: Adriatica Editrice, 1950, 22pp.
Gives a rapid review (pp. 3-4) of various scholarly approaches to aspects of *AN.* Stresses the light yet highly diversified quality of the work, "un gioco vario eppur compatto". Its general character is that of fable or dream rather than realistic narrative; the pervasive but delicate irony detracts from the epic spirit and at the same time contributes to the idyllic mode employed. A sensitive and persuasive reading.

1951

72 Cohen, Gustave. "Une curieuse, etc." *Studi Medievali*, n.s., XVII (1951), 114-23.
Virtually identical with C66. This time, slight changes in wording and a few more examples.

73 Rogger, Karl. "Etude descriptive de la chantefable *Aucassin et*
73a *Nicolette.*" *ZRP*, LXVII (1951), 409-57; LXX (1954), 2-58.
Agrees with a number of critics who consider the last part of the *chantefable* (after XVII) inferior to the first; unlike them, Rogger attempts to give facts to show that the work is made up of heterogeneous parts. The study is lengthy, full of detail, bristling with statistics concerning word-counts and stylistic devices. The latter do not necessarily lead the reader to the same conclusions concerning a second author. The study is less than convincing on a number of counts.
Review: .1 M. Roques, *R*, LXXVI (1955), 113-19. (Reasserts the thesis of single authorship.)

1951-2

74 Spitzer, Leo, "*Aucassin et Nicolette* Line 2, Again." *MP*, XLVIII (1951-2), 154-6.

A response to Grace Frank's criticism (C67) of C64. Spitzer remains persuaded that *deport* means "conduct"; if, however, it has its more usual meaning, it must signify "heroic exploit" and double the *proueces* of 1. 6. Alas! This meaning of *deport* is quite as unattested in 13th-century literature as is the other. This matter, as well as *viel* (*mel*?) *antif*, remains unsettled.

1952

75 Gennrich, Friedrich. "Chanson de geste." In *Die Musik in Geschichte und Gegenwart.* Kassel and Basel: Bärenreiter, 1952, II, cols 1081-4.

An examination of the way the *chansons de geste* were probably performed, with special consideration of the melodies appearing in the MS of *AN.* By a change of melody the composer marks the arrival of the concluding verse of each *laisse.*

76 Thomov, Thomas S. "Les Groupements de substantifs, verbes et adjectifs et leurs effets rythmiques dans les strophes d'*Aucassin et Nicolette.*" In *Mélanges de linguistique et de littérature romanes offerts à Mario Roques.* Paris: Didier, 1952, pp. 289-302.

Examines the technique of accumulation, much used in *AN*; these groups of two, three, or four words, belonging to the same part of speech, give a peculiar rhythm to much of the verse. A perceptive study.

1954

77 Frank, Grace. *The Medieval French Drama.* Oxford: Clarendon Press, 1954.

Ch. XXIII (pp. 237-42) treats *AN*. Frank includes it in a study of dramatic literature to emphasize the narrow line separating narrative material, often recited or read aloud, and works intended for the stage. Postulates that *AN* was written for two performers (singer and narrator), both of whom spoke the dialogues. Includes plot summary and comment on form, sources, and tone.

73a See C73.

78 Henry, Albert. *Chrestomathie de la littérature en ancien français.* 2 vols. Berne: Francke, 1954.

Gives the excerpts from *AN* under the rubric "littérature dramatique" (pp. 272-8), and calls it a "mime, chanté et récité par un seul acteur". Uses the MS and the Roques 1929 edition (Aa25).

79 Roques, Mario. "Deux notules sur des passages contestés du manuscrit d'*Aucassin et Nicolette*."*R*, LXXV (1954), 520.
In *AN*, XIV, 15-22, Roques maintains the reading "en son oeul" of his edition (Aa24, 25), against Suchier's correction "en son l'oeul"(Aa8, etc.), and shores it up with a similar formula in Marguerite de Navarre. As for XXIV, 64-9, "or tien...vint que j'ai ci", it is not necessary to correct this to read "vint sous"; the ellipsis is similar to that in other works where specific sums of money are mentioned.

1955

80 Connor, Wayne. "The Loge in *Aucassin et Nicolette.*" *RR*, XLVI (1955), 81-9.
Emphasizes the impracticality of the *loge* as a shelter; Nicolete, in fact, does not use it as such. It is the "lair of the precious 'beast'" that N. in her message tells A. to hunt. It is also a love test (will A. stop when he sees it?), and this is because it symbolizes her (A. calls her *flors de lis* twice in XL). The message of the *loge* is "your *fleur de lis* is here". Another problem is the troublesome *erbe du garris* of XIX, 13. Connor suggests a scribal error for *larris* (=moor), while leaving the question open.

81 Lefèvre, Y. "Sur *Aucassin et Nicolette*, IV, 8." *R*, LXXVI (1955), 93-4.
When Count Garin orders the Viscount, Nicolete's adoptive father, to send her away, the MS reads "se je le puis$_7$ avoir". This $_7$ (=*et*) is usually omitted in the editions. Lefèvre proposes a scribal error; the MS from which our copy was made might have had *iaveir*, with the first *i* badly written and an *e* that was read as an *o*. L. reconstructs the original thus: "se je le puis ja veir", and puts it into context as follows: "Faites disparaître Nicolette, qu'on ne la voie plus. Si je la vois encore, je la ferai brûler." An attractive hypothesis.

82 Roques, Mario. "Corrections." *R*, LXXVI (1955), 99-102.
In two parts: 1. "Corrections et additions au tirage et au supplément de 1936" (Aa30); 2. "Additions à la bibliographie critique (publications postérieures à 1936)".

1956

83 Brunel, Clovis. "'Etoilete je te voi que la lune trait a soi'." *R*, LXXVII (1956), 510-14.
An explanation of the astronomical phenomenon referred to in *AN*, XXV: when Venus appears to be close to the moon, their apparent approach to each other is visible to the naked eye. Thus the moon seems to draw the planet. A minor point, but persuasive. Summarized, C84.

84 Brunel, Clovis. "L'Etoilette invoquée dans *Aucassin et Nicolette*." In *Comptes rendus de l'Académie des Inscriptions et Belles-Lettres* (1956), p. 334.
A summary of C83.

85 Pelan, Margaret, ed. *Floire et Blancheflor.* Publications de la Faculté des Lettres de l'Université de Strasbourg. Textes d'Etude, V. 2nd ed. Paris: Société d'Edition "Les Belles Lettres", 1956.
Takes up (pp. xxv-xxvi) the relationship between *FB* and *AN*, mentioning critics who have held that *AN* is based on a lost earlier version of *FB*, and others who postulated a lost common source. Pelan believes that Scheludko (C40) may be right in thinking that the two authors were quite independent of each other. A judicious, though brief, note.

1957

86 Van der Veen, J. "Les Aspects musicaux des chansons de geste." *Neophilologus*, XLI (1957), 82-100.
Gives a few pages (89-91) to *AN*, largely repeating in abridged form the suggestions of Gérold and Chailley (C47, 56, 65) for the adjustment of lines of verse to the musical phrases. The music of *AN* is here reproduced with errors in the transcription of the first phrase.

1958

87 Aarburg, Ursula. "Die Laissenmelodie zu *Aucassin et Nicolette*." *Musikforschung*, XI (1958), 138-43.
Argues that the concluding short melody is wrongly written in the MS, and should be transposed upward a fifth so that it begins on the same note that concludes the longer, repeated tune. Other medieval melodies are offered by way of justification. Interesting, though not conclusive.

1959

88 Micha, Alexandre. "En relisant Aucassin et Nicolette." *MA*, LXV (1959), 279-92.
Takes up impressively the defense of the last part of the work (from XXVII onward), against the criticisms of Paris, Foerster, Meyer-Lübke, Bédier, and Rogger (C10, C12, C17, Ba6, C73, 73a). Micha considers that this part is of a piece with the rest: the same poetic irony prevails, the same turn of mind is in evidence.

89 Pelan, Margaret. "Le Deport du viel antif." *Neuphilologische Mitteilungen*, LX (1959), 180-5.
Reviews other scholars' attempts to define *deport* by reference to other medieval and later texts and concludes that although *se deporter* can

mean *se comporter*, a noun *deport* in the moral sense of "conduct" is still merely conjectural. Pelan postulates a scribal error of *deport* for *depart*, a well-attested noun meaning "separation". *AN* does not have it elsewhere, but thrice uses the verb *departir* (=*séparer*). The reading *deport* is clear in the MS; but in other words this scribe frequently made his a's and o's indistinguishable from one another. The proposed translation of the opening lines: "If anyone would like to hear good stanzas / about the separation by the very old man / of two pretty youngsters..." Ingenious and not improbable.

1960

90 Jodogne, Omer. "La Parodie et le pastiche dans *Aucassin et Nicolette*." *Cahiers de l'Association Internationale des Etudes Françaises*, XII (1960), 53-65; rpt in *Der altfranzösische höfische Roman.* Ed. Erich Köhler.Wege der Forschung, CDXXV. Darmstadt: Wissenschaftliche Buchgesellschaft, 1978, pp. 289-300.

A very solid and penetrating study of the parodic techniques of *AN*. Basically, there are three: "le jeu permanent du contre-pied, l'exagération et la bouffonerie". With parody goes pastiche: *AN* follows in its content the idyllic romance of the *Floire et Blanchefleur* type. Other literary forms (lyric poetry, *chanson de geste*) are also suggested.

91 Rohr, Rupprecht. "Zu den Laissen in *Aucassin et Nicolette*." *Romanistisches Jahrbuch*, XI (1960), 60-80.

A meticulous and exhaustive examination of the patterns of assonance, rime, alliteration, and word-repetition in the verse sections of *AN*. Rohr draws attention to the frequency of rime within the generally assonanced *laisses.*

1961

92 Coppin, Joseph. *Amour et mariage dans la littérature française du nord au moyen-âge.* Paris: Librairie d'Argences, 1961.

On pp. 88-91, an analysis of the nature of the love between Aucassin and Nicolete: ingenuous, sentimental, obsessive yet innocent, it is the typical passion of the idyllic romance.

93 Tiemann, Hermann. *Die Entstehung der mitterälterlichen Novelle in Frankreich.* Hamburg, 1961, 22pp.

On pp. 21-2, takes *AN* as an example of how flexible the short narrative had become and how it could incorporate elements previously limited to other genres.

94 McKean, M. Faith. "Torelore and Courtoisie." *RN*, III, 2 (Spring, 1962), 64-8.

Stresses the abnormality of the relationship of hero and heroine, while they are moving in the real world; Nicolete plays the masculine, Aucassin the feminine rôle. Only in the unreal milieu of Torelore does A. become heroic and decisive, while N. becomes passive. That they revert to their former rôles after leaving Torelore, having learned nothing from the experience, is an example of the author's irony. A slight but sensible note.

1963

95 Monsonégo, Simone. "Contribution statistique à l'étude de l'emploi des mots dans *Aucassin et Nicolette*." *Bulletin des Jeunes Romanistes*, VIII (1963), 37-42.

A highly technical and statistical exposition of a thesis that will be developed in book length in C103.

1963-4

96 O'Gorman, Richard F. " 'Vint que j'ai.' An Example of Ellipsis in Old French?" *RN*, V (1963-4), 85-7.

Agrees with the common emendation of XXIV, 67, to read "or tien, fait Aucassins, vint [sous] que j'ai ci en me borse".

1964

97 Guiraud, Pierre. "L'Opposition actuel-virtuel. Remarques sur l'adverbe de négation dans *Aucassin et Nicolette*." In *Mélanges de linguistique romane et de philologie offerts à M. Maurice Delbouille.* Gembloux: Duculot, 1964, I, pp. 295-306.

Proposes that, like works in Modern French, *AN* uses adverbial particles (e.g. *pas, point, mie*) not to reinforce the negation but to actualize the verb. These particles are etymologically positive; their use or non-use in negative propositions allows the author to distinguish between the actual and the virtual. A useful insight, if accurate.

1965

98 Colby, Alice. *The Portrait in Twelfth-Century French Literature: An Example of the Stylistic Originality of Chrétien de Troyes.* Geneva: Droz, 1965.

Refers to *AN* specifically only on p. 29; but the observations on conventional beauty and ugliness have general validity for the 13th c. as well as the 12th.

99 Griffin, Robert. "*Aucassin et Nicolette* and the Albigensian

Crusade." *Modern Language Quarterly,* XXVI (1965), 243-65.
Believes that *AN* bears witness to a connection between the Albigensian heresy and the poetry of the troubadours. Nicolete is associated with beauty, light, and healing; she and her lover pass through something akin to *endura* and *consolamentum* before achieving perpetual union; A.'s preference for Hell with, rather than Heaven without, his beloved, recalls the expressions of certain troubadours. The battle of Beaucaire in *AN* may be based on the real siege, in 1216. Count Garin's failure to keep his word to A. is similar to Raymond VI's abjuration of Catharism. Much of this fails to convince.

100 Kaminska, Alexandra. "La Valeur des pronons personnels 'en' et 'y' dans *Aucassin et Nicolette*, chantefable du moyen âge." *Revue de Linguistique Romane*, XXIX (1965), 98-104.
A study, rather derivative, of these pronouns as representative of ideas or whole clauses or sentences.

101 Woods, William S. "The 'aube' in *Aucassin et Nicolette*." In *Mediaeval Studies in Honor of Urban Tigner Holmes, Jr.* Ed. John Mahoney and John Esten Keller. UNCSRLL, LVI. Chapel Hill: University of North Carolina Press, 1965, pp. 209-15.
Examines the scene of the watchman's warning and the lovers' separation. Although this passage has been called a dramatized *aube*, it differs from the usual *aube* in many respects. Woods considers these departures from the norm to be intended for comic effect. The suggestion is not improbable.

1966

102 Harden, Robert. "*Aucassin et Nicolette* as Parody." *SP*, LXIII (1966), 1-9.
Traces an evolution in scholarship from the time when *AN* was held to be a naïve tale of idyllic love. To develop this theory, scholars had to pass over or explain away some unheroic actions of the hero and some embarrassing situations, such as that in Torelore. Aucassin, by his childishness, ineptitude, and lack of enterprise, is a veritable anti-hero. The whole work recalls, in language and tone, the *fabliau*; it mocks revered personages and types, as well as the idyllic romance generally. Interesting and informative on the evolution of *AN* scholarship.

103 Monsonégo, Simone. *Etude stylo-statistique du vocabulaire des vers et de la prose dans la chantefable 'Aucassin et Nicolette.'* Bibliothèque Française et Romane, Série A: Manuels et Etudes Linguistiques, X. Paris: Klincksieck, 1966. 154pp.

A study, bristling with tables and indices, of the vocabulary of the verse and prose sections of *AN*. According to Monsonégo, the results show a considerable difference, the parts in verse having a higher proportion of nouns and adjectives than those in prose, while the latter give prominence to verbs and adverbs. The vocabulary of the verse tends to be conventional, in conformity with the diverse lyric genres represented; that of the prose is freer, more varied, closer to that of everyday life. One would need to verify these results before agreeing or disagreeing with the conclusions drawn.

Reviews: .1 B. Blakey, *Western Canadian Studies in Modern Languages and Literatures*, II (1970), 88-94. See C113.
.2 C. Camproux, *RLR*, LXXVII (1967), 241-3.
.3 J.J. Duggan, *RPh*, XXIII (1969-70), 253-4.
.4 B. Folkart, *SF*, XIV (1970), 126.
.5 R.-L. Wagner, *Bulletin de la Société de Linguistique de Paris*, LXII, 2 (1967), 45-6.

104 Owen, D.D.R. "*Aucassin et Nicolette* and the Genesis of *Candide*." *Studies on Voltaire and the Eighteenth Century*, XLI (1966), 203-17.

A statement and development of the hypothesis that Voltaire drew on *AN* extensively and systematically in writing *Candide.* Owen shows that Sainte-Palaye's modernized edition of *AN* (Ba1) was available by 1756 and that Voltaire knew and admired Sainte-Palaye. It is probable (though not proved) that Voltaire had read *AN* by the time he began *Candide.* Owen's attempt to show that he drew on it, and that the parallels between the two tales are too many to be caused by coincidence, is not entirely convincing, since it stresses resemblances and glosses over differences.

105 Knott, Eleanor, and Gerard Murphy. *Early Irish Literature.* London: Routledge and Kegan Paul, 1966.

Contains some discussion (pp. 37, 161-2) of the alternation of prose and verse in narrative fiction, which appears comparatively late in Irish literature but is common there by the 12th century. The *Acallam* cycle of anecdote-ballads has affinities with *AN*. Marginal, but interesting.

1967

106 Martin, June Hall. "The Problem of Parody and Three Courtly Lovers: Aucassin, Troilus, and Calisto." Diss. Emory University, 1967. 223pp.

Summarized in *Dissertation Abstracts*, XXVIII (1967-8), 4136-7A. Revd version published as C124.

1968

107 Blakey, Brian. "*Aucassin et Nicolette*, XXIV, 4." *FS*, XXII (1968), 97-8.

Treats the *desu* in "a painnes peust on nouer desu el plus entier". In the MS the word is indistinct. Using an ultra-violet photograph, Blakey reads *de scu* (=*d'escu*), and takes the passage to mean "so that one could hardly have tied up a crown in the largest remaining piece of his clothing". The *escu* began to be minted in 1266-70; if *d'escu* is not a scribal intervention but the author's choice, it would suggest a later date for *AN* than has hitherto been supposed.

108 Smith, Barbara. "Toward an Interpretation of *Aucassin et Nicolete*." *Rendezvous*, III, 1 (1968), 43-59.

A student essay.

1969

109 Fónagy, Ivan and Judith. "Sur l'ordre des mots dans *Aucassin et Nicolette*. Projection synchrone d'un changement." *Bulletin de la Société de Linguistique de Paris*, LXIV, 1 (1969), 101-3.

Attempts to study the shift from the normal Old-French order of predicate-subject, object-verb (with decreasing semantic tension) to the contrary tendency in classical French. Takes the verse sections of *AN* as representing *gravis* or *mediocris stylus*, the prose parts as *humilis stylus* (without explanation) and finds the older, decreasing order prevailing in the first, the increasing order in the second. Takes an 1892 translation (unidentified) as representing *le français classique*. A study of little if any value.

110 Ménard, Philippe. *Le Rire et le sourire dans le roman courtois en France au moyen âge (1150-1250).* Université de Paris, Faculté des Lettres et Sciences Humaines. Geneva: Droz, 1969.

Numerous short references, informative though scattered (and indexed) to *AN*: the rude *vilain*, Aucassin's foolish behaviour, Nicolete's disguise as a *jongleur*, Torelore, the word *rire*, the nature of the parody, the gaiety and humour of the whole work, the use of exaggeration in personal descriptions, the paradox of A.'s preference for Hell.

1969-70

111 Clevenger, Darnell H. "Torelore in *Aucassin et Nicolette*." *RN*, XI (1969-70), 656-65.

A rather general examination of the work and the way the Torelore episode divides it into two parts, the first marked by a mixture of reality, fantasy, and folklore, the second showing an illogical or mysterious causality. The king and queen suffer from "love-sickness" and love is the ultimate butt of the satire – not all love, however, but misguided love, represented by the king and queen and also to a degree by the protagonists. Not entirely convincing since the author of *AN* speaks not of the sentiments of Torelore's rulers but only of the custom of the land.

112 Sargent (-Baur), Barbara Nelson. "Parody in *Aucassin et Nicolete*: Some Further Considerations." *FR*, XLIII (1969-70), 597-605.

Examines two passages, Aucassin's Hell-Paradise speech and the description of Nicolete, and finds parody of rhetorical conventions and a certain perversity of thought and expression in the first. The second, while conventional in itself, is out of the normal place for such portraits both in works of literature and in the prescriptions of, e.g., Matthieu de Vendôme.

1970

113 Blakey, Brian. "Some Problems of Method in the Statistical Analysis of Literary Texts, with Special Reference to S. Monsonégo's *Etude...*" *Western Canadian Studies in Modern Languages and Literatures*, II (1970), 88-97.

Subjected Monsonégo's research (C103) to a computer and found the results of the original study unreliable. His conclusion: the approach is good in theory, faulty in practice.

114 Goetinck, G.W. "*Aucassin et Nicolette* and Celtic Literature." *Zeitschrift für celtische Philologie*, XXXI (1970), 224-9.

Examines some features of *AN* that are reminiscent of Celtic literary traditions (mixture of prose and verse, a large and ugly character encountered in a wood, a sea voyage culminating in a visit to a land of strange customs). Finds, though, no proof of direct influence of Breton *conteurs* on the author of *AN*. An article more speculative than enlightening.

115 Jodogne, Omer. "*Aucassin et Nicolette, Clarisse et Florent.*" In *Mélanges de langue et de littérature du moyen âge et de la renaissance offerts à Jean Frappier.* Publications Romanes et Françaises, CXII. Geneva: Droz, 1970, I, pp. 453-81.

A detailed comparison of *AN* with *Clarisse et Florent*, often proposed as an imitation of *AN.* Jodogne considers phonology at the assonance, morphology, general story line, succession of episodes, characters, textual similarities and differences. Conclusion: *AN* is not only a pastiche of popular epic and romance in general but an imitation and parody of a specific work, *CF*. An important and challenging study.

116 Liborio, Mariantonia. "*Aucassin et Nicolette*: i limiti di una parodia." *Cultura Neolatina*, XXX (1970), 156-71.

The abundant use of formal rhetorical conventions suggests that the author was a learned person writing for an audience acquainted with the *arts poétiques*. Literary circles were a meeting ground for both courtly traditions and irreverent, "bourgeois" attitudes; such a circle, Liborio thinks, is hinted at by the use of *roi* in Aucassin's Hell-Paradise speech (*roi*=presidents of *puys*). *AN* is a parody of a serious tale (real or imaginary). It is a *divertissement* bearing on literature, not on society, for all social institutions represented are, at the end, unchanged. Some of these positions are sound; but there is much speculation as well.

117 Owen, D.D.R. *The Vision of Hell: Infernal Journeys in Medieval French Literature.* Edinburgh: Scottish Academic Press, 1970.

AN comes up (pp. 193, 198-9) in a discussion of visits to Hell by kings and heroes. Owen suggests that Aucassin's Hell-Paradise speech may have inspired the passage in *Baudouin de Sebourc* in which the traitor Gaufroi calls this world a Paradise if one is rich and Hell if one is poor. The resemblances noted seem very slight.

118 Payen, Jean-Charles. *Le Moyen Age.* I:*Des origines à 1300.* Littérature Française. Paris: Arthaud, 1970.

Places *AN* under the rubric "Le roman idyllique" (pp. 172-3), while noting that it lends itself to dramatic presentation with several voices. Stresses the links between prose and verse parts, which recall the *laisses similaires* of French epic. Calls the work an "anti-roman", Aucassin an "anti-héros", the setting a "monde démythifié". Sees it as basically a serious work, a condemnation of folly, a "sottie avant la lettre". There are some stimulating insights here.

119 Regnier, Claude. " 'Le mellor de mes bues, Roget, le mellor de me carue' (*Aucassin et Nicolette*, éd. M. Roques, XXXIV, 51-52)." In *Mélanges de langue et de littérature du moyen âge et de la renaissance offerts à Jean Frappier.* Publications Romanes et Françaises, CXII. Geneva: Droz, 1970, II, pp. 935-43.

Insists, convincingly, that the *carue* of the hideous peasant Aucassin meets in his wanderings is not a plow, as Roques and other editors have stated, but rather the team of oxen that the peasant usually drove.

120 Vance, Eugene. "The Word at Heart: *Aucassin et Nicolette* as a Medieval Comedy of Language." *Yale French Studies*, XLV (1970), 33-51.

Situates *AN* in the context of medieval speculation on the nature of language, stimulated by the realist-nominalist controversy. In the 12th and 13th centuries, as vernacular literature was coming into its own, writers were increasingly preoccupied with matters of expression. Verbal action was replacing physical action. Vance ingeniously proposes that the author of *AN* may have intended to create a comedy of language as well as a comedy of love.
Review: .1 J. Enquehard, *SF*, XVI (1972), 124-5.

1971

121 Ch'en, Li-Li. "*Pien-wen*, Chantefable and *Aucassin et Nicolette.*" *Comparative Literature*, XXIII (1971), 255-61.
Pien-wen, i.e. "a narrative depicting the marvelous incident of..." is part of the titles of some MSS discovered in Tun-huang in 1900. Some of these tales alternate prose and verse and use a single rime in the verse sections. Of these *chantefables*, several have verse sections using seven-syllable lines and ending in five-syllable lines. Some of them, like *AN*, begin with prologues stressing the beneficial effect of hearing the tale that is to follow. But the influence of *pien-wen*, possibly through Arabic intermediaries, is only conjectural, as the author admits.

1972

122 Dorfman, Eugene. "The Flower in the Bower: *garris* in *Aucassin et Nicolette*." In *Studies in Honor of Mario A. Pei.* Ed. John Fisher and Paul A. Gaeng. UNCSRLL, CXIV. Chapel Hill: University of North Carolina Press, 1972, pp. 77-87.
An exposé of the hypothesis that *AN* is a complex of secret messages from a Jew to his co-religionists in a time of post-Albigensian persecution. The lilies adorning Nicolete's bower (*loge*) are both her "signature" and that of the Shulamite in the Song of Songs. Dorfman finds significant resemblances in descriptions contained in both works. However, when passages in *AN* differ from key sections in the Song of Songs, he postulates deliberate inversion. This is a method that can be used to prove anything.

123 DuBruck, Edelgard. "The Audience of *Aucassin et Nicolete*: Confidant, Accomplice, and Judge of its Author." *Michigan Academician*, V (1972), 193-210.
Sees in *AN* an attack on upper-class ideals in an effort to please the common man. Most of the characters are commoners; even Nicolete's foster parents are burghers, as "their property is in the city". N., escaping from her tower, "descends into what seems to be a burgher's

garden" (because "the only flower mentioned is the humble marguerite" – but cf. the rose in V, 12). The courtly/bourgeois dichotomy, by now largely discredited, receives little support from the arguments brought forth here.

124 Martin, June Hall. *Love's Fools: Aucassin, Troilus, Calisto, and the Parody of the Courtly Lover.* Colección Támesis, A, XXI. London: Tamesis, 1972.

Sums up in Ch. I some recent critical positions concerning courtly love and gives an overview of how, according to medieval theorists and *romanciers*, a lover feels and ought to behave. Ch. II (pp. 23-36) measures Aucassin against this standard. Noting the inversion of rôles of hero and heroine, Martin holds this to be an aspect of a larger category: incongruity. The hero is an exaggerated courtly lover in a world of practical considerations and unromantic people. This is "humorous parody". A sensible, learned, competent study. See C106.

Reviews: .1 J.M. Aguirre, *Bulletin of Hispanic Studies*, LII (1975), 94-6.
.2 A.D. Deyermond, *FS*, XXX (1976), 186-7.
.3 K.V. Kish, *RPh*, XXIX (1975-6), 344-6.
.4 M. Thiry-Stassin, *MA*, LXXXI (1975), 157-8.
.5 K. Whinnom, *MLR*, LXVIII (1973), 144-5.

125 Stratman, Carl J. *Bibliography of Medieval Drama.* Berkeley: University of California Press, 1954; 2nd ed. New York: Ungar, 1972.

The second edition includes two pages (II, pp. 767-9) of listings for *AN*.

126 Zink, Michel. *La Pastourelle: poésie et folklore au moyen âge.* Paris: Bordas, 1972.

On pp. 67-8, takes Aucassin's Paradise-Hell speech as illustrative of the distance between Christian and courtly doctrine, an *amoralisme* that marks popular poetry as well as that of the troubadours and trouvères.

127 Zumthor, Paul. *Essai de poétique médiévale.* Paris: Editions du Seuil, 1972.

Discusses *AN* on pp. 429-31 in connection with "dialogue et spectacle". Stresses the theatricality of all medieval poetry, intended as it was for public recitation. Postulates the use of dialogue when more than one *jongleur* was performing, and draws attention to the "dialogue virtuel" implied in some works. Zumthor considers *AN* either a dialogue-and-narrative composition or a dramatic monologue. This is a shrewd look at the realities of medieval literary communication and at the limited validity of modern concepts of genre.

1973

128 Juneau, Marcel, "L'énigmatique 'waumoné' dans *Aucassin et Nicolette.*" *ZRP*, LXXXIX (1973), 447-9.
Treats the unorthodox weapons of Torelore, *poms de bos waumonés. AN* is the only medieval text showing the meaning "overripe" (the modern meaning in the North and East of France, where it is spelled *gaumoné*). Postulates a derivation from Middle-Dutch *walm* (=bale of straw) to *waumoné* (=mouldy like old straw, hence old, spoiled). Finds an analogy in *chaume, chaumir,* to grow mouldy. Von Wartburg's *Französisches etymologisches Wörterbuch* needs to be corrected on this point. A persuasive argument.

129 Schøsler, Lene. *Les Temps du passé dans 'Aucassin et Nicolette.'* Etudes Romanes de l'Université d'Odense, V. Odense: University Press, 1973. 121pp.
A study of the simple past, compound past, imperfect, and historical present. It takes up direct discourse in prose, direct discourse in verse, narration in prose, and narration in verse. A careful, highly technical analysis.
Reviews: *.1 C.W. Aspland, *Journal of the Australasian Universities Languages and Literature Association*, XLIII (1975), 124-5.
.2 B. Folkart, *SF*, XIX (1975), 122.
.3 P. Rickard, *FS*, XXXII (1978), 308-9.
.4 S.N. Rosenberg, *MLN*, XCII (1977), 840-2.
.5 M. Sandeman, *RF*, LXXXVII (1975), 698-700.
.6 M. Wilmet, *Revue Belge de Philologie et d'Histoire,* LVI (1978), 215-17.

130 Stevens, John. *Medieval Romance: Themes and Approaches.* London: Hutchinson University Library, 1973.
On pp. 129-30, a discussion of *AN* in the context of religion and romance. The *cantefable* flaunts romance values by opposing them to Christian ones in the Hell-Paradise speech. Stevens treats the *mais que* of VI, 24 and 38 inconsistently (first "unless", then "provided"); the force of Aucassin's paradoxical assertion is thus diminished. Stevens holds that the blasphemy does not necessarily imply any commitment on the author's part; it is merely part of the absurdity of young love. A shrewd and balanced commentary.

131 Williamson, Joan B. "Naming as a Source of Irony in *Aucassin et Nicolette.*" *SF*, LI (1973), 401-9.
Treats the application of the principle of reversal to the names and characters of the two lovers. A French Christian hero has an Arabic name, a Spanish Saracen heroine has a French one. Repetition of these

names with unnecessary frequency reminds the hearer/reader of their incongruity, and Aucassin's Arabic name goes well with his unorthodox views. One or two details call for reservations.

1973-4

132 Rea, John A. "The Form of *Aucassin et Nicolette*." *RN*, XV (1973-4), 504-8.

Finds parallels to the prose-and-song of the *cantefable* in the *vidas* and *razos* of the troubadours. These were also made up of sung lyrics interspersed with narrative passages in prose, and intended for public presentation. Transitional formulas between *vidas* and *razos* resemble some in *AN.* One may have certain reservations (e.g. concerning "troubadour origin" of ideal female beauty as embodied in Nicolete). The formal resemblances, however, are striking.

1974

133 Baader, Renate. "Ein Beispiel mündlicher Dichtung: *Aucassin et Nicolette*." *Fabula*, XV (1974), 1-26.

Stresses the aspects of *AN* that suggest the affiliation with oral composition. The *laisses*, in particular, show traits recalling the formulaic technique of the *chansons de geste* ("easy" assonances on identical parts of speech; three- and four-syllable formulae to fill the lines). The prose sections also show oral influence: parataxis, hypotaxis, conventional epithets, repetitions of descriptive and narrative motifs, sequential structure, accumulations, a fondness for superlatives. All these point toward a sort of composition that was initially oral, improvised, and derived from *Märchen*. This article contains some up-to-date bibliography and judicious comments on recent studies.

134* Dorfman, Eugene. "The Lamp of Commandment in *Aucassin et Nicolette*." *Hebrew University Studies in Literature*, II (1974), 30-72.

135 Schneiderman, Leo. "Folkloristic Motifs in *Aucassin et Nicolette*." *Connecticut Review*, XIII (1974), 56-71.

A study (by a psychologist) based on Bourdillon's 1887 translation. Gives a résumé containing a number of errors of fact, and not entirely corresponding with the following analysis. The latter dwells heavily on ritual (rather than medieval European civilization). Nicolete's confinement in the tower, e.g., is a form of ritual isolation; she is ineligible for marriage because of ritual impurity; the twelve wounds she receives while crossing the moat are a symbolic reference to the menstrual periods of the year and their associated rites of isolation and purification. The real substance of the tale is the "rites of passage from adolescence to sexual maturity". It may be so, but the reasons adduced here are insufficient to prove it.

136 Thiébaux, Marcelle. *The Stag of Love: The Chase in Medieval Literature*. Ithaca: Cornell University Press, 1974.
Studies *AN* (p. 104) in the context of hunting imagery common in vernacular literature from the late 12th century. Considers, oddly, that each of the lovers sees the other as a hunter.

1975

137 Owen, D.D.R. *Noble Lovers.* London: Phaidon; New York: New York University Press, 1975.
Some pages (136-44, 169, 170) on *AN*; basically a summary of the tale, with a translation of some passages. The *enfans petis* of I, 3 is rendered "little children"; the two occurrences of *mais que* of the Paradise-Hell speech come over first as "unless" and then as "so long as". Owen succeeds in conveying the freshness and vivacity of the tale, and some of its caricatural side.

138 Rossman, Vladimir J. *Perspectives of Irony in Medieval French Literature.* The Hague: Mouton, 1975.
Pp. 95-106 deal with *AN.* The study is marred by an imperfect knowledge of Old French (e.g. IX, 13, of Aucassin's feet, "bien li sissent es estriers" rendered "the stirrups suited him well"; in XII, Nicolete demonstrates "ingenuity as well as physical strength" by climbing down her improvised rope while holding up her skirt fore and aft). The conclusions as to irony, based on such readings, do not inspire confidence.

139 Szabics, Imre. "Moyens syntaxiques de l'expressivité poétique dans la chantefable *Aucassin et Nicolette.*" *Acta Litteraria Academiae Scientiarum Hungaricae*, XVII (1975), 427-41.
Stresses the subordination of subject and theme to verbal expression in the Middle Ages. Concentrates on syntactic and stylistic procedures, seen as aids in the amplification of themes, motifs, and key words. Separate sections treat verb tenses (especially the compound past), word order (as used for emphasis), comparisons (often original), metaphors, and antithesis. Brilliant, sensitive, erudite, richly provided with notes.

140* Szabics, Imre. "Az *Aucassin és Nicolette* expresszív szerkezetei." *Filológiai Közlöny*, XXI (1975), 137-53.

1976

141* Clark, S.L., and Julian Wasserman. "Wisdom Buildeth a Hut: *Aucassin et Nicolette* as Christian Comedy." *Allegorica*, I (1976), 250-68.

142 Trotin, Jean. "Vers et prose dans *Aucassin et Nicolette.*" *R*, XCVII (1976), 481-508.

A penetrating examination of the distribution of three key words and their etymological families: *ami(e), biax/bele, doux/douce*, the frequent use of which in *AN* contributes to the formulaic quality of both prose and verse. There follows a study of how these semantic fields serve to link the prose narration and the *laisses.* The subtlety and variety of the linkings mirror the complexity of the *laisse-récit* alternation.

1976-7

143 Stewart, Joan Hinde. "Some Aspects of Verb Use in *Aucassin et Nicolette.*" *FR*, L (1976-7), 429-36.

Following Monsonégo's observations (C103) on the number and prominence of verbal forms in *AN*, Stewart concentrates on a single passage (IV). The remarks on the frequent use here of the imperfect subjunctive (rare in Modern French) contribute nothing new; in any case, so short a passage does not lend itself well to statistical analysis. Stewart's stress on the expressive use of verb tenses does, on the other hand, produce some perceptive *explications de texte.*

1977

144* Cali, Francesco. " 'C'est d'Aucassin et de Nicolete': beauté et poésie d'une idylle amoureuse 'du viel antif'." *Culture Française* (Bari), XXIV (1977), 99-108.

145* Dorfman, Eugene. "The Sacred and the Profane in *Aucassin et Nicolette.*" In *Homenaje a Robert A. Hall, Jr.: Ensayos lingüísticos y filológicos para su sexagésimo aniversario.* Ed. by David Feldman. Madrid: Playor, 1977, pp. 117-31.

146* Hower, Caroline F. "*Aucassin et Nicolette.*" In *The Alfred C. Howell Collection. A Bibliography.* Ed. Louis Silverstein. New York: Vassar College Bookstore, 1977.

147 Hunt, Tony. "Precursors and Progenitors of *Aucassin et Nicolette.*" *SP*, LXXIV (1977), 1-19.

Stresses that the author did not invent a new literary form, but exploited two literary precedents: the *prosimetrum* of Late Antiquity (beginning with Martianus Capella's *De Nuptiis Philologiae et Mercurii* and Boethius's *De Consolatione Philosophiae*, familiar to educated medievals) and the vogue, apparently begun by Jean Renart, of inserting sung lyrics into a vernacular narrative. A well-informed and persuasive study.

1978

148 Bellanger, Yvonne. "*Aucassin et Nicolette* ou le charme discret de l'insoumission." *Stanford French Review*, II (1978), 47-50.

A slight piece concentrating (in a very conversational style) on the Torelore episode; it draws a good deal on Pauphilet's *Legs du moyen âge* (C70). *AN* is intended for a popular audience, hence the mockery of courtesy and the knightly caste. In Torelore "cette dérision est portée à son paroxysme" – surely an exaggeration.

149* Cartwright, Sarah. "*Aucassin et Nicolette*. Essai d'application de la méthode de Propp." *Les Bonnes Feuilles*, VII, 1-2 (Spring, 1978), 85-101.

150* Hattaway, John. "Cateron." In *Mélanges de philologie romane offerts à Charles Camproux*. Montpellier: Université Paul-Valéry, Centre d'Estudis Occitans, 1978, I, pp. 383-4.

1979

151 Hunt, Tony. "La Parodie médiévale: le cas d'*Aucassin et Nicolette*." *R*, C (1979), 341-81.

A vigorous challenge to the now widely-held idea that *AN* is parodic in whole or in part. From the source, identified as Urban T. Holmes, Jr (Bb11), this interpretation is followed downstream, with attention to Micha (C88), Jodogne (C90, 115), Harden (C102), Monsonégo (C103), Clevenger (C111), Liborio (C116), Sargent (C112), Vance (C120), Martin (C124), Williamson (C131), Woods (C101), and Rogger (C73). Some of these critical positions are here represented with less nuance than is found in their full exposition, so that what has been proposed as conjecture is reported as firm assertion. The two crucial uses of *mais que* (*AN* VI) are interpreted in two ways, with reference to *mais* in the same passage (but cf. *mais que* in XXVII, 14, not mentioned by Hunt). Considers *AN* a *conte populaire* and a *pot-pourri*, devoid of parodic intent but containing satire of contemporary chivalry, i.e. its frame of reference is not literary but social; the work was composed for a bourgeois audience. Since the audience of *AN*, real or potential, remains unknown, Hunt's conclusions (based largely on hypothetical audience expectation and reaction) appear no more conclusive than those positing parodic intention on the author's part.

AUTHOR INDEX

Apuleius C37

Bayle, Pierre C17
Boccaccio C37
Boethius C35, 147

Chrétien de Troyes C14

Dante C37

Herodotus C53, 66
Hippocrates C53
Homer C32

Jean Renart C147

Machiavelli C17
Marguerite de Navarre C79
Martianus Capella C37, 147
Matthieu de Vendôme C112
Menippus C37

Parthenius C41
Petronius C37
Plutarch C66

Seneca C35, 37
Sidney, Sir Philip C37

Varro C37
Virgil C35
Voltaire C104

TITLE INDEX

Acallam C105
Aeneid C35
Agassin et Virelette Be

Baudouin de Sebourc C117

Candide C104
Celestina C124
Chevalier de la charrete C14
Clarisse et Florent C115
Conte du Graal C14

De Beneficiis C35
De Consolatione Philosophiae C146
De Nuptiis Philosophiae et Mercurii C37, 146
Dictionnaire historique et critique C17

Erec C14

Floire et Blancheflor C5, 24, 26, 33, 85, 90

Guillaume de Dole C147

Ismir et Etoilette p. 8

Marcassin et Tourlourette p. 8, Be

Odyssey C32
One Thousand and One Nights C34

Piramus et Tisbé C29

Satire Ménippée C37
Siège de Barbastre C36.1
Song of Songs C63, 122

Thidreks Saga C41
Troilus and Criseyde C124

"Ward and Prince Uns, Tale of" (in *One Thousand and One Nights*) C34

SUBJECT INDEX

Accentuation C31
Albigensian Crusade C99, 122
Antecedents C37, 41, 72, 121, 146
Anti-hero(ine) C102, 118, 148
Anti-roman C118
Arabic influence C33, 37, 39, 49, 121, 131
Arabic literature C19
Arts poétiques C112, 116
Assonance C16, 27, 91, 115, 133
Aube C63, 101
Audience C123, 148, 151

Calisto C124
Cantefable (see also *prosimetrum*) C62, 121, 132
Carue C119
Catharism C99
Celtic literature C19, 37, 53, 105, 114
Chansons de geste C22, 90, 118, 133
Chinese literature C121
Christianity C126
Comic character C101, 110, 120
Courtoisie C12, 94
Couvade C53, 66, 72, 111
Cryptology C122
Cues C19, 46, 46.1

Dating C14, 19, 20, 27, 107
Description (see also Portrait) C1, 110, 112, 133
Dialect C14
Dramatic character C10, 19, 30, 46, 77, 78, 118, 125, 127
Dual authorship C73

Fabliau C102
Fille biche C43
Folklore C33, 43, 53, 111, 123, 133, 135
Formulae C38, 46, 46.1, 133, 140

Geography C58

Hell C1, 17, 53, 110, 112, 116, 117, 126, 130
Hunting imagery and motifs C41, 43, 136

Idyllic romance C71, 90, 92, 102, 118, 144
Irish literature: see Celtic literature
Irony C26, 71, 88, 94, 131, 138

Jewish authorship C122

Laisses C47, 58, 64, 91, 118, 133
Language, theories of C120
Latin sources C29, 35, 37, 147
Loge C80, 122
Love C12, 92, 106, 124
Lyric C90, 99, 103, 143

Marriage C92
Mime C21, 62, 78
Melodies C18, 22, 42, 60, 75, 86, 87

Names C39, 131
Negation C97
Norse literature C37, 41
Nouvelle C20, 93

Oral character C10, 133
Oriental sources C33, 35, 40, 41, 121

Paradise C1, 17, 53, 112, 116, 117, 126, 130
Parody C14, 70, 90, 94, 101, 102, 110, 112, 115, 116, 124, 137, 151
Pastiche C90, 115
Pastourelle C126
Philosophy C120
Picard dialect: see Dialect
Pien-wen C121
Portrait (see also Description) C98
Prologue C12, 25, 59, 64, 67, 68, 89, 121
Propp method C149
Prosimetrum C30, 37, 105, 121, 132, 140, 147

Puy C116

Razos (and *vidas*) C132
Regional origin of author C11, 14, 19, 49, 52, 54, 66
Rhetoric C112, 116
Rhythm C76
Rime C91
Rire C110
Rites of passage C135

Scythians C53
Social satire C123, 151
Stage-directions C19, 30, 46.1
Statistical analysis C73, 95, 103, 113
Syntax C6, 9, 38, 109, 139

Torelore C94, 110, 111, 148
Troilus C124

Unity C28, 73, 73.1, 88

Verb tenses C129, 139, 143
Vers orphelins C16, 22
Vidas (and *razos*) C132
Vocabulary C52, 95, 103, 139, 142

INDEX OF CRITICS, EDITORS, REVIEWERS, TRANSLATORS

Aarburg, U., C87
Acher, J., C18
Adams, H., C12
Aguirre, J.M., C124.1
Arpád, T., Bd6
Aschner, S., C21
Aspland, C.W., C129.1

Baader, R., C133
Bar, F., C63
Beck, J.B., C22, 27.1
Bédier, J., Ba6; C85, 88; p. 13
Bellanger, Y., C148
Bida, A., Aa7; Ba5; Bb2; C3; p. 7
Blakey, B., C103.1, 107, 113
Blondheim, D.S., C17
Boselli, A., Bd7
Bourdillon, F.W., Aa10, 12, 15, 20, 21, 26, 40; Ab1; Bb1, 3, 5, 6, 7, 13; C10; pp. 7, 15-19
Brandin, L., C23
Brunel, C., C83, 84
Brunner, H., C5, 11
Bülow, E. von, Bc2

Cali, F., C144
Camproux, C., C103.2
Cartwright, S., C149
Chailley, J., C65, 86
Chatelain, Y., C54
Ch'en, Li-Li, C121
Clark, S.L., C141
Clédat, L., Aa24.1
Clermont, R., Be
Clevenger, D.H., C111, 151
Cohen, G., Ba11; Be; C66, 72
Colby (-Hall), A., C98
Connor, W., C80
Coppin, J., C92
Cormier, R.J., Be
Coulon, M., Ba9
Counson, A., Aa14, 16, 17, 19, 23, 29
Crescini, V., C13, 15, 25

Decroos, J., Bd4
Delvau, A., Aa6; Ba4
Deyermond, A.D., C124.2
Dockhorn, R., C28
Dorfman, E., C122, 134, 145
DuBruck, E., C123
Dufournet, J., Aa41; Ba13; pp. 15, 17-19
Duggan, J.J., C103.3

Eldridge, C.D., Bb11
Elliott, A.M., Aa9.1
Enquehard, J., C120.1

Faral, E., C29
Fauriel, C., Ba3; C1
Feilitzin, H. von, Bd11
Foerster, W., Aa14.1; C14, 15, 87, 88
Folkart, B., C103.4, 129.2
Fónagy, I., C109
Fónagy, J., C109
Foulet, L., C38
Frank, G., C46, 48, 67, 74, 77

Gennrich, F., C75
Gérold, T., C47, 56, 86
Gibb, E.J.W., Bb5
Goetinck, G.W., C114
Goldberg, L., Bd5
Goodrich, N.L., Bb12
Gourmont, R. de, Ba1
Griffin, R., C99
Guiraud, P., C97
Guiton, P.A., Ba7
Gundlach, F., Bc4

Hale, E.E., Bb7
Hansmann, P., Bc7
Harden, R., C102, 151
Hattaway, J., C150
Heiss, H., C30
Henry, A., C78
Henry, M.S., Bb6
Héricault, C. d', Aa5
Hertz, W., Bc3
Holk, A., Bd2
Holmes, U.T., Bb11; C151
Hower, C.F., C146
Housman, L., Bb8
Hunt, T., C147, 151

Ideler, J.L., Aa4

Jenkins, T.A., Aa24.2
Jodogne, O., C90, 115, 151
Johnston, O.M., C24
Jordan, L., C34, 40
Juneau, M., C128

Kaminska, A., C100
Kish, K.V., C124.3
Knott, E., C105
Koch, J., Aa9.2; C5.1
Kopaczynski, W., Bd8
Krappe, A.H., C35, 41

La Curne de Sainte-Palaye, J.B. de, Aa31; Ba1, 2; Bc2; Be; C101
Lang, A., Bb4, C7
Lefèvre, Y., C81
Legrand d'Aussy, J.B., Aa3; Ba2; Bb1
Lerch, E., Aa22.1, 27.1; C34
Leskovak, M., Bd10
Levy, R., C57, 68
L'Hôpital, M., Be
Liborio, M., C116, 151
Linker, R.W., Aa32, 35
Liveroskaia, Mme, Bd9
Lot-Borodine, M., C26
Lubert, Mlle de, p. 8

Macdonough, R., Bb2
Martin, J.H., C106, 124, 151
Mason, E., Bb9
Massias, G., Be
Matarasso, P., Bb13
McKean, M.F., C94
Ménard, P., C110
Méon, D., Aa1, 2, 3, 4; Ba3; Bb9; C3; p.14
Meyer-Lübke, W., C19, 30, 87, 88
Micha, A., C88, 151
Michaut, G., Ba6
Michaëlis, S., Bd3
Mohl, J., Ba3
Moland, L., Aa5, 6; Bb9
Mombello, G., Aa41.1
Monsonégo, S., C95, 103, 113, 151
Morf, H., Aa17.1
Mosher, T.B., Bb3, 4
Moyer, E.F., Bb11
Murphy, G., C105
Mussafia, A., C3

Neri, F., C44, 48

O'Gorman, R.F., C96
Oppeln-Bronikowski, F., Bc8
Orr, J., C52.1
Orsini, L., Bd7
Owen, D.D.R., C104, 117, 137

Paris, G., Aa7, 8.1, 13.1; Bb2, 6; Bc3; C4, 10, 11, 85, 88; pp. 7, 14, 18
Pater, W., C1, 2
Pauphilet, A., Aa33; Ba8; C70, 148
Payen, J.C., C118
Pelan, M., C85, 89
Piccoli, R., C16
Pons, M., Ba12; C149

Raimondo, C., Bd7
Raynaud, G., Aa8.2
Rea, J.A., C132
Reese, G., C60
Régnier, C., C119
Reinhard, J.R., C37
Rickard, P., C129.3
Rieger, E., Bc9
Riffard, L., p. 8

Rogger, K., C73, 73a, 85, 88, 151
Rohr, R., C91
Roques, M., Aa24, 25, 30, 31, 36, 37, 38, 39, 42; Ba8, 11; Bb12, 13; C36, 36.1, 44.1, 46.1, 48, 49.1, 50, 51, 52.2, 55, 63, 69, 73.1, 78, 79, 82; pp. 7, 15-18
Rosenberg, S.N., C129.4
Rossman, V.J., C138
Rousse, M., Aa41.2

Sadron, P., Be
Sallwürk, E. von, Bc5
Sandeman, M., C129.5
Sansone, G.E., C71
Sargent (-Baur), B.N., C112, 151
Sauter, H., C52
Sauvageot, M., Be
Schäfenacker, P., Bc6
Scheludko, D., C33, 34, 40, 85
Schlickum, J., C6
Schneiderman, L., C135
Schøsler, L., C129
Schultz-Gora, O., C61
Schulze, A., Aa11.1, 13.2; C11, 59
Sedaine, J.-M., Be; p. 8
Settegast, F., C32
Smirnov, A.A., Bd9
Smith, B., C108
Söderhjelm, W., C20
Spitzer, L., C64, 67, 74
Stengel, E., Aa8.3; C64
Stevens, J., C130
Stewart, J.H., C143
Storost, W., C42
Stratman, C.J., C125
Suchier, H., Aa7.2, 8, 9, 11, 13, 14, 14.1, 16, 17, 19, 22, 23, 27, 28, 29; Ba6; Bb5, 6, 12, 13; C4, 8, 11, 14, 15, 50, 64, 79; pp. 7, 14-20
Suchier, W., Aa22, 24.3, 27, 28; C31, 34, 39
Szabics, I., C139, 140

Tanquerey, F.J., C45, 50
Thiébaux, M., C136
Thiry-Stassin, M., C124.4
Thomas, A., Aa16.1
Thomov, T.S., Aa34; Bd11; C76
Thomson, E.W., Bb6
Thureau, G., C27
Thurneysen, R., C9
Tiemann, H., C93
Tobler, A., Aa8.4; C4, 11
Tournoux, G.A., Aa18
Trotin, J., C142

Urwin, K., C58

Van der Veen, J., C86
Vance, E., C120, 151
Velten, H.F., C43
Vendryès, J., C53
Vollmöller, K., Aa9.3

Wagner, R.L., C103.5
Wasserman, J., C141
Waters, E.G.R., Aa21.1
Way, G.L., Bb1
Weber, E., Aa9.4
West, M., Bb10
Whinnom, K., C124.5
Williams, E.B., Ba10
Williams, J.K., C48, 49
Williamson, J., C131, 151
Wilmet, M., C129.6
Wilmotte, M., Aa11.2
Winkler, E., C62
Wolff, O.L.B., Bc1
Woods, W.S., C101, 151

Zink, M., C126
Zumthor, P., C127

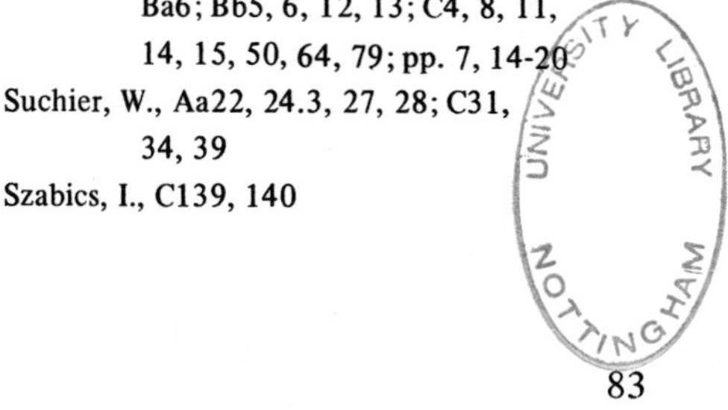

RESEARCH BIBLIOGRAPHIES & CHECKLISTS

Edited by

A.D.Deyermond, J.R. Little and J.E.Varey

1.	Little, R.	Saint-John Perse: a bibliography for students of his poetry, 1971 Supplement no. 1, 1976
2.	Sheringham, M.	André Breton: a bibliography, 1972
3.	Sharrer, H.L.	Hispanic Arthurian Material in the Middle Ages: a critical bibliography, I, 1977
4.	Hoy, P.	Julien Gracq: essai de bibliographie, 1938-1972, 1973
5.	Little, J.P.	Simone Weil: a bibliography, 1973 Supplement no. 1, 1979
6.	Labriolle, J. de	Claudel and the English-speaking World: a critical bibliography, 1973
7.	Scott, J.W.	Madame de Lafayette: a selective critical bibliography, 1974
8.	Wright, B.	Eugène Fromentin: a bibliography, 1973
9.	Wells, M.B.	Du Bellay: a bibliography, 1973
10.	Bradby, D.	Adamov, 1975
11.	Aquila, A.J.	Alonso de Ercilla y Zúñiga: a basic bibliography, 1975
12.	Griffin, N.	Jesuit School Drama: critical literature, 1976
13.	Crosby, J.O.	Guía bibliográfica para el estudio crítico de Quevedo, 1976
14.	Smith, P.	Vicente Blasco Ibáñez: an annotated bibliography, 1976
15.	Duggan, J.J.	A Guide to Studies on the *Chanson de Roland*, 1976
16.	Bishop, M.	Pierre Reverdy: a bibliography, 1976
17.	Kelly, D.	Chrétien de Troyes: an analytic bibliography, 1976
18.	Rees, M.A.	French Authors on Spain, 1800-1850: a checklist, 1977
19.	Snow, J.T.	The Poetry of Alfonso X, el Sabio: a critical bibliography, 1977
20.	Hitchcock, R.	The *Kharjas*: a critical bibliography, 1977
21.	Burgess, G.S.	Marie de France: an analytical bibliography, 1977
22.	Bach, K.F. and G. Price	Romance Linguistics and the Romance Languages: a bibliography of bibliographies, 1977
23.	Eisenberg, D.	Castilian Romances of Chivalry in the Sixteenth Century: a bibliography, 1979
24.	Hare, G.	Alphonse Daudet: a critical bibliography I. Primary material, 1978 II. Secondary material, 1979